Kim Campbell Thornton

Bloodhounds

Everything about Purchase,
Care, Nutrition, Breeding,
Behavior, and Training

With 50 Full-Color Photographs

Illustrations by Michelle Earle-Bridges

BARRON'S

Acknowledgments

The author's thanks go to the Bloodhound people who so generously gave their time and photos to this book—Dr. John and Susan Hamil, James L. Ryan, Jack Shuler, Roger Caras, Gretchen Schultz, Camille McArdle, DVM—and to the many other writers of fiction and nonfiction who have made dogs, and especially the Bloodhound, their subject.

Cover Photos

Toni Tucker: Front cover, inside front cover; Judith E. Strom: Back cover; Paola Visintini: Inside back cover.

All inquiries should be addressed to:
Barron's Educational Series, Inc.
250 Wireless Boulevard
Hauppauge, NY 11788

http://www.barronseduc.com

International Standard Book No. 0-7641-0342-3

Library of Congress Catalog Card No. 98-10542

Library of Congress Cataloging-in-Publication Data
Thornton, Kim Campbell.
    Bloodhounds : everything about purchase, care,
  nutrition, breeding, behavior, and training / Kim
  Campbell Thornton ; illustrations by Michele
  Earle-Bridges.
        p.   cm.—(A complete pet owner's manual)
    Includes bibliographical references (p. 93) and
index.
      ISBN 0-7641-0342-3
    1. Bloodhound. I. Earle-Bridges, Michele. II. Title.
III. Series.
SF429.B6T48   1998
636.753'6—dc21   98-10542
                                                  CIP

Printed in Hong Kong

9 8 7 6 5 4 3 2 1

The Author

Kim Campbell Thornton is the former editor of *Dog Fancy* magazine, which during her tenure won three Dog Writers Association of America Maxwell Awards for best all-breed magazine. Since beginning a new career as a freelance writer, she has written seven books about dogs and cats as well as a number of articles for various animal-related publications. She serves on the Board of Governors of the Dog Writers Association of America and on the board of the Dog Writers Educational Trust. A longtime admirer of the hound breeds, she shares her home with a 12-year-old retired racing Greyhound named Savanna.

Photo Credits

Scott McKiernan/ZUMA: pages 4, top bottom; 5; 17; 20, top, bottom; 25; 28 top; 52 bottom; 53 top; Paola Visintini: pages 8; 9; 13, top, bottom; 16; 21; 28 bottom; 36, top, bottom; 37; 40; 41; 48 top, bottom; 49; 52 top; 53 bottom; 60 top left; 64; 69; 73; 76; 80; 84; 88; Nance, pages 29; 45; 60 top right, bottom left, right; 61 top left, right, bottom left, right; Kent and Donna Dannen, page 33. Photos of paintings on page 12 courtesy of William Secord Gallery, New York, New York.

Important Notes

This pet owner's guide tells the reader how to buy and care for a Bloodhound. The author and the publisher consider it important to point out that the advice given in the book is meant primarily for normally developed puppies from a good breeder—that is, dogs of excellent physical health and good temperament.

Anyone who adopts a fully grown dog should be aware that the animal has already formed its basic impressions of human beings. The new owner should watch the animal carefully, including its behavior toward humans, and should meet the previous owner. If the dog comes from a shelter, it may be possible to get some information on the dog's background and peculiarities there. There are dogs that for whatever reason behave in an unnatural manner or may even bite. Under no circumstances should a known "biter" or an otherwise ill-tempered dog be adopted or purchased as a pet or show prospect.

Caution is further advised in the association of children with dogs, in meeting with other dogs, and in exercising the dog without a leash.

Even well-behaved and carefully supervised dogs sometimes do damage to someone else's property or cause accidents. It is therefore in the owner's interest to be adequately insured against such eventualities, and we strongly urge all dog owners to purchase a liability policy that covers their dog.

Contents

Entreaty, humor, and stubbornness are all facets of the Bloodhound personality.

Preface

The Bloodhound is a legendary dog. It is one of the few breeds whose history can truly be traced for more than 1,000 years, yet it is not a breed that is well known. There are many misconceptions about Bloodhounds, often to their detriment. Many people—not because they are criminals—fear the sight of them. They are perhaps victims of tales that Bloodhounds are vicious, their jaws dripping with saliva as they contemplate tearing to pieces anyone they sniff out.

Nothing could be further from the truth. The people who know and love Bloodhounds unanimously describe them as lovable critters, good buddies, delightfully good natured and jolly with a good sense of humor, tolerant, and affectionate. While their size—which also comes as a surprise to many—and their deep bark are intimidating, they are more likely to slobber intruders with kisses than to bite them. The Bloodhound is a dog that is serious about its work, yet it's always ready for a good time. Rarely will you find a Bloodhound with the temperament of a crank.

That's not to say, however, that the Bloodhound is the perfect pet. Indeed, it has been bred to be just the opposite: a dog that thinks for itself and likes to be in charge. It's big and sprawling and smelly, and once it picks up a scent, it thinks of nothing else save tracking down its source, heedless of cars or dinner or brambles or the person stumbling along at the other end of the leash.

This book is an introduction to life with a Bloodhound, a dog whose world is defined by its nose. If you are thinking of purchasing a Bloodhound, or have recently acquired one, it will help you understand and live in harmony with your new companion. In the following pages, you'll find tips on training, grooming, nutrition, and health care, along with color photos and descriptive illustrations. As well as being a guide to Bloodhound ownership, we hope this book will also be a keepsake that you will treasure and turn to again and again over the years with your special dog.

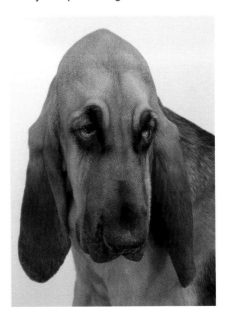

History of the Bloodhound

The Early Scenthound

Most dog breeds as we know them today have been in existence for less than 200 years. Before the mid-nineteenth century, few people recorded the bloodlines of dogs. Their main concern was whether a dog was good at what it did: hunting, herding sheep, pulling a cart, or guarding the home. A dog that excelled in its work was bred so that it could pass on its good qualities. It was not until Victorian times that people who bred dogs began to take an interest in standardizing appearance as well.

Although specific breeds did not exist 2,000 years ago, there were several different types of dogs, each performing an important function. One of the oldest and best known of these types was the hound, of which there were two kinds: sighthounds and scenthounds. Sighthounds were fleet-footed and sharp of eye, while scenthounds were slower, relying on a powerful sense of smell and unflagging tenacity to track their prey.

The scenthound of ancient times had characteristics that have remained the same over the centuries, even though the dog has changed in other ways. It was a large dog—though probably not as large as Bloodhounds today—with long ears and loose skin. The pendulous ears and folds of skin helped sweep the scent up toward the sensitive nose, while the dog's size enabled it to bring down large game.

The first-century Roman naturalist Pliny the Elder wrote of dogs called Segusii, that "discover and trace out the tracks of the animal, leading by leash the sportsman who accompanies it straight up to the prey. And as soon as ever it has perceived it, how silent it is and how secret but significant is the indication which it gives, first by the tail and afterward by the nose." In his book *Historia Animalium,* third-century writer Claudius Aelianus (Aelian) makes mention of a tenacious type of hound whose scenting powers were unparalleled by those of any other dog. This hound would not give up the trail until it had located its prey, Aelian reported. Who can doubt that these hounds of antiquity were the progenitors of the dog we know today as the Bloodhound, a breed that has been described as the modern representative of the oldest race of hounds that hunt by scent?

Such a dog could not be kept a secret. It spread throughout the world, eventually arriving in Constantinople, from whence it made its way to Europe.

Blooded Hounds in Medieval Europe

It is dawn at the edge of the Ardennes Forest. As the rising sun glistens off the early morning dew, the horses paw the earth impatiently, and the hounds, 200 in number, strain at their leads. Colorful banners wave in the breeze, and the bells hanging from the ladies' surcoats jingle softly. Finally, the huntsman blows his horn and the dogs set to work, using their powerful noses to track the wild boar.

Riding to hounds was an important part of medieval and Renaissance society, especially in France and Italy. Even bishops and other church dignitaries, who ranked with the nobility, threw themselves wholeheartedly into the ritual of the hunt. Many abbeys kept packs of hounds and bred fine dogs in their kennels. It is from the care taken with their bloodlines that dog historians believe the Bloodhound took its name—it was a "blooded," or aristocratic, breed.

St. Hubert Hounds

The forerunner of today's Bloodhound was the eighth-century St. Hubert hound, named for the man who molded it into his ideal hunting dog: François Hubert. The young Hubert, born to a noble family, was a passionate hunter. Even after his wife died and he retired to a monastery at Mouzon in the Ardennes on the border of what are now Belgium and France, Hubert continued to hunt and to breed his dogs. They were valued for their ability to follow a "cold," or old, trail, and to contend with large, dangerous, wounded animals such as wild boar, deer, and European bison.

After Hubert's death, he was canonized, becoming known as the patron saint of hunters. St. Hubert became so associated with hunting and with the dogs of his breeding that November 3, St. Hubert's Day, is celebrated with a blessing of the hounds, especially in the countries where hunting and fine dogs are still revered: Belgium, France, and Ireland.

The abbots who followed after St. Hubert kept up the tradition of breeding the fine dogs. They were so successful that in place of the usual tribute, the King of France accepted three pairs of hounds from the abbey each year. They were highly prized as gifts, indicating as they did the mark of the king's favor, and being possessed of such great scenting prowess.

The first St. Hubert hounds were black, later developing coloration of black and tan. Other scenthounds of this time that contributed to the development of the St. Hubert hound were the grayish Southern hounds and the white Talbot hounds, which are depicted in Italian frescoes and paintings.

The fame of the St. Hubert hound spread across the sea to England, thanks to William the Conqueror, who brought some of the dogs with him when he claimed the English throne in 1066. Other English monarchs also favored the breed. Elizabeth I was an enthusiastic huntswoman and kept packs of St. Hubert hounds, as did her favorite, the Earl of Essex, who maintained a pack of 800 hounds. Johannes Caius, an English physician and dog lover who lived during Elizabeth's time, wrote about the breed, suggesting that its name could be attributed to the belief that the dogs followed the scent of their prey's blood. "For that reason," he wrote, "they are properly called Sanguinaraii [derived from the Latin word for blood]." It is clear that Dr. Caius is writing of a Bloodhound-like dog; he describes it as being large, with drooping lips and ears. Besides its supposed ability to track prey through the scent of blood (an incorrect assumption), Dr. Caius credited this hound with being able to follow dry human footsteps for long distances, find people in large crowds, and track its prey across water. Shakespeare, too, mentions a dog that sounds greatly like the Bloodhound. In "A Midsummer Night's Dream," Theseus says:

"My hounds are bred out of the Spartan kind,
So flew'd, so sanded; and their heads are hung
With ears that sweep away the morning dew;
Crook-knee'd, and dew-lapp'd like Thessalian bulls;
Slow in pursuit, but match'd in mouth like bells . . ."

The Bloodhound's powerful nose and never-say-die attitude make it the best known tracker and mantrailer in the world.

From its eighth-century beginnings, the St. Hubert hound flowered in Renaissance France. The French nobles looked upon the hound as the highest form of dog. Indeed, hounds are to France as terriers are to England. But in the late eighteenth century, 1,000 years after St. Hubert began shaping the breed, the French Revolution changed everything.

Back from the Brink of Extinction

After the French Revolution, the great estates were in ruins, and many members of the aristocracy had fled to England or America. The days of the great hunts were gone, and the St. Hubert hound faced a future that seemed to hold no place for such an anachronistic breed. As with so many breeds, the destruction of vast expanses of forest and the subsequent disappearance of large game animals almost brought about the extinction of the blooded hound. Fortunately, dog lovers in England recognized that the Bloodhound, as it came to be known in that country, had value beyond its skills as a hunter.

For one, it was used to help create new breeds. The development of faster hounds with keen noses was aided by crosses with Bloodhounds. The Beagle, Foxhound, and Harrier can all thank the Bloodhound for their sharp sense of smell. And as Dr. Caius had noted, it was recognized that the Bloodhound had exceptional tracking skills that could be used on man or beast, on land and over water. There was a reason that the Bloodhound was sometimes called the sleuth hound, in recognition of its prowess in tracking poachers and other criminals. A Bloodhound in pursuit of a thief was permitted to follow a trail wherever it led, even into people's homes. Stories of Bloodhounds being used to track transgressors date to the sixteenth century, but it wasn't until 1805 that the Thrapthon Association for the Prevention of Felons, a law enforcement organization, made the first recorded use of Bloodhounds to track down poachers and thieves. But even this valuable contribution to society might not have been enough to save the breed without the intervention of two other factors: the curiosity of the Victorians and the rise of the middle class.

The Victorian Era

The Victorian era, which stretched from 1837 to 1901, was a time of great exploration and societal change. British explorers and military men brought back oddities—including dogs—from around the world. And a new class of people had developed. No longer was there only the rich and the poor. Now there was a middle class, a group of people with disposable income and leisure time, which they used to mimic, as nearly as possible, the lifestyles of the wealthy. One such aspect they adopted was the desire to own fine or unusual animals.

It was during this time that purebred dogs as we know them today began to be developed. Breeds whose numbers had dwindled almost to the point of disappearance were resurrected by the Victorian craze for the unusual. The Bloodhound was one of these. Dog shows sprang up, with the first one taking place in 1859, so that people could show off the results of their breeding programs. Even Queen Victoria entered one of her Bloodhounds in a dog show in 1869. Without the advent of dog shows, the patronage of Queen Victoria—who brought many dog breeds into fashion—and the Bloodhound's growing reputation as a mantrailer, it might well have faded into history, its great scenting ability only a memory.

Instead, it was taken up not only by the queen but also by wealthy dog fanciers, including the Baron Rothschild and Lord Faversham. From dogs of their breeding came Druid, the breed's first champion, bred by T. A. Jennings. Jennings and two other gentlemen, Major Cowen and J. W. Pease, bred the top-winning Bloodhounds in England until 1868, when they started getting competition from other breeders, such as Edwin Brough. Brough is considered the father of the modern Bloodhound because of his contribution in writing the first standard for the breed in collaboration with Dr. Sidney Turner. Today's American standard remains closer than any other to that original standard.

The British also conducted the first mantrailing trials with Bloodhounds in 1898. The trials, promoted by the Association of Bloodhound Breeders (which celebrated its 100th anniversary in 1997), soon caught on as a sport and led to greater use of the dogs in law enforcement. Today, English Bloodhound owners compete for the Brough Cup, in which the dogs follow a trail that is a minimum of six hours old and must choose from a group of people the person who laid the trail. The Bloodhounds work off lead, with their handlers following on horseback.

Not surprisingly, the Bloodhound also found its way to America, as early as colonial times. The breed had its ups and downs in this country, but now it is firmly established, and American breeders produce some very fine dogs.

In many European countries the Bloodhound is known as the Chien de St. Hubert—*or like these Italian Bloodhounds, the* Cane di St. Uberto—*after its creator.*

The Bloodhound in America

Perhaps the first mention of the Bloodhound in early America was made by Benjamin Franklin in 1764. In a letter to Richard Jackson, he mentioned wanting to acquire "Fifty couple of true Bloodhounds" to assist in tracking down Indians who were plundering settlements and kidnapping people. It isn't known whether he succeeded in his quest, but it is likely that at least some Bloodhounds were brought to the colonies both for hunting and tracking.

Once again, however, a war laid the Bloodhound low. A stage version of Harriet Beecher Stowe's antislavery novel *Uncle Tom's Cabin* falsely put the dogs in the role of slavering beasts that viciously ran down escaped slaves. The Bloodhound's reputation was soiled by the dramatic license, and many Bloodhounds, including a pack owned by Confederacy President Jefferson Davis, were killed because of it.

The breed did not recover until 1888, when Edwin Brough brought three Bloodhounds from England to compete in a show hosted by the Westminster Kennel Club. Interest in

The false image of ferocious Bloodhounds tracking down escaped slaves was created by a stage version of Harriet Beecher Stowe's novel Uncle Tom's Cabin.

the Bloodhound was rekindled, and several American breeders acquired the dogs. Still, Bloodhounds were not many in number, and few were used in mantrailing, being owned by gentlemen who kept them purely for sport or companionship.

Prominent American breeders in the early twentieth century included Geraldine Rockefeller Dodge and veterinarian Leon F. Whitney. Dodge's Giralda Farm Kennel produced many fine Bloodhounds that contributed to the bloodlines of today's dogs, and Dr. Whitney was known for his training of mantrailers. His book on the subject was well read by handlers of trailing Bloodhounds.

Bloodhounds are still relatively rare in this country today, which is just how their fanciers like it. Only 2,057 Bloodhounds were registered with the American Kennel Club in 1996, giving the breed a registration ranking of 60 out of the 141 breeds AKC registered that year. In contrast, 149,505 Labrador Retrievers—the number one breed—were registered.

The Bloodhound in Art, Literature, Film, and Pop Culture

Before the camera came along to record every aspect of human life, including the magnificence of dogs, people relied on artists to capture images of what was important to them. And it's clear that dogs were important, even in the very earliest civilizations. Assyrian hounds, which may have been the forebears of the modern Bloodhound, were carved on a stone slab that was dated to the seventh century B.C. Medieval tapestries included hounds in their depictions of the hunt. But perhaps the classic era of dog portraiture was the nineteenth century, when artists such as Sir Edwin Landseer, Maud Earl, and Ward Binks put on canvas the finest sporting dogs of the time, including many Bloodhounds. Early nineteenth-century paintings of Bloodhounds by Sydenham Edwards and Philip Reinagle do not resemble in the least the dogs we know today, but by mid-century they had begun to take on their modern appearance, as evidenced by the paintings of John Sargent Noble, who was known for his paintings of the breed.

Perhaps one of the most famous works featuring a Bloodhound is Landseer's *Dignity and Impudence,* painted in 1839, which shows a bemused Bloodhound sharing a doghouse with a small terrier. An 1852 painting by E. Grimstead depicts a Bloodhound head, and Maud Earl's *Brought to Bay* (1898) shows three of Edwin Brough's Bloodhounds, Chs. Barbarossa, Babbo, and Benedicta. A painting by Briton Riviere, *Requiescat,* (1889) uses a Bloodhound to explore the concept of fidelity, a quality for which the dog has long stood. In this painting, which harkens back to medieval times, a knight in armor is laid out on his deathbed, attended only by his faithful Bloodhound, who sits at attention, gazing nobly upon his dead master. Later, in the 1930s, Reuben Ward Binks painted many of the dogs owned by Geraldine Rockefeller Dodge, including her Bloodhound Ch. Brigadier of Reynalton.

Bloodhounds have also been popular in twentieth-century media such as film and television, although they are often portrayed inaccurately. Like the pre-Civil War-era stage productions, the 1927 film version of *Uncle Tom's Cabin* depicted Bloodhounds as vicious, as did a number of prison-escape movies, including *I Am a Fugitive From a Chain Gang* with Paul Muni, *The Defiant Ones* with Tony Curtis and Sidney Poitier, and *Cool Hand Luke* with Paul Newman. These films gave new meaning to the term

Who Put the Blood in Bloodhound?

American humorist and essayist James Thurber often wrote about dogs and featured them in his wry cartoons. About how the Bloodhound got its name, he had this to say in his essay "Lo, Hear the Gentle Bloodhound": "My own theory is that the 'blood' got into the name because of the ancient English superstition that giants and other monsters, including the hound with the Gothic head and the miraculously acute nose, could smell the blood of their prey. The giant that roared, 'I smell the blood of an Englishman!' had the obscene legendary power, in my opinion, to smell blood through clothing and flesh. . . . It seems to me . . . that legend and lore are more likely than early breeders to have given the Bloodhound his name."

The Bloodhound was used to create or improve several breeds, including the Beagle, Foxhound, and Harrier.

The Captive, *John Sargent Noble, English, 1848–1896, oil on panel.*

Brigadier, *R. Ward Binks, English, 1880–1950, gouache on paper.*

"hounded." Movies that feature a more lighthearted image of Bloodhounds are *Bloodhounds on Broadway, Shirley Valentine,* and *Cooper and Dudley,* not to mention the Disney animated movie *Lady and the Tramp,* which includes the character Trusty the Bloodhound.

One of the most inaccurate portrayals of a Bloodhound was that of Duke on the television show *The Beverly Hillbillies.* When many people think of Bloodhounds, lazy old Duke is the dog that comes to mind, giving rise to the mistaken belief that the dogs are easygoing and need little exercise.

Clover and Pensive at Play, *1934, R. Ward Binks, gouache on paper.*

Brigadier, *1935, R. Ward Binks, gouache on paper.*

The Bloodhound is ever-curious, always wanting to know what that interesting smell is.

In more recent television history, a Bloodhound appears in the sitcom "Dave's World" and in the animated show "King of the Hill." Other images of the Bloodhound in pop culture include commercials for Snapple beverages and Mazda trucks; McGruff the Crime Dog, whose public service announcements urge viewers to "Help take a bite outta crime"; and numerous portrayals in print and animated cartoons, which usually feature them as judges, detectives, solemn, pipe-smoking characters, or Southern "good ole boys."

Bloodhounds have fared rather better in the written word. Among the books about Bloodhounds are *Yankee: The Inside Story of a Champion Bloodhound* by naturalist and television commentator Roger Caras, *Manhunters! Hounds of the Big T* by Lena Reed and Bill Tolhurst, and a series of mysteries

The breed has captured the imagination of readers, movie-goers, and couch potatoes.

And hark! and hark! the deep-
   mouthed bark
Comes nigher still and nigher:
Bursts on the path a dark Blood-
   hound,
His tawny muzzle tracked the
   ground,
And his red eye shot fire.

—Sir Walter Scott
from *The Lay of the Last Minstrel*

by Virginia Lanier: *Death in Bloodhound Red, The House on Bloodhound
Lane,* and *A Brace of Bloodhounds.*
Lanier's stories are set in Georgia's
Okefenokee Swamp area, where her
protagonist, Jo Beth Sidden, breeds
and trains Bloodhounds for use in law
enforcement. Lanier accurately por-
trays the Bloodhound's foibles as well
as its master scenting powers.

That Sense of Smell

Why does the Bloodhound have
such a powerful nose? Well, first let's
take a look at how scent and the
sense of smell work. Scent is given off
with every move we make. The body
throws off flakes of dead skin that
carry the unique odor of each human
being. That odor, which is affected by
what we eat, our genetic heritage,
how often we bathe, and the shampoo, deodorant, and perfume we use,
is formed when the bacteria on the
skin cells release unique volatile substances. Bloodhounds can detect
these fatty acids emitted from the skin
surface or from surfaces or objects
that have come in contact with the
fatty acids. Depending on the weather
or climate, the scent trail stays near
the ground (cool or damp conditions)
or rises up into the air (warm to hot
conditions). Bloodhounds can not only
follow a scent on the ground, they can
also air-scent; that is, they can follow
a scent that has risen from the

ground. Because the scent drifts with
the breeze, the dog doesn't necessarily follow its quarry in a direct line.

But what makes the Bloodhound
such a master at following the scent
trail? Earlier, we talked about its size,
long ears, and loose skin. All of these
factors play a role in the Bloodhound's
ability to nose out its quarry. The
entire length of the Bloodhound's
head is 12 inches (30 cm) or more in
males, 11 inches (28 cm) or more in
females. With that long head comes a
wide foreface and a nose with large,
open nostrils. Because the dog's
headpiece is so large, there is more
room in the nasal cavity for *turbinates,*
bony plates containing specialized
cells that continuously feed sensory
information about odors to the olfactory nerve, which runs directly to the
brain, where the odor information is
processed. A Bloodhound could have
as many as 200 million of these cells
working for it, compared to only five
million or so for humans. People have
only about 1 square inch (2.5 cm) of
olfactory membrane, while Bloodhounds may have an olfactory membrane of 22 square inches (56 cm).

The power of the nose is aided by
the Bloodhound's long ears and the
loose skin that forms a cape, or cup,
around its head and neck. The ears
sweep the scent up toward the nose
and the cape traps it for further reference. Even the Bloodhound's propensity for drooling may play a role, with
the heat from the saliva creating
steam, causing the scent to rise.
Finally, the Bloodhound's tenacity
makes it a superior trailing dog. Long
after other dogs are ready to drop, the
Bloodhound keeps going and going
and going.

The Bloodhound as Companion

It takes a special person to own a
Bloodhound. You will hear that said
about every breed, and for each breed

it is true, but for different reasons. In the case of the Bloodhound, there are a number of factors to consider when deciding if you are that special person who should take one home.

Size. Bloodhounds are large. They can stand more than two feet (61 cm) tall at the withers and can weigh more than 100 pounds (45 kg). They are not quarrelsome, but their size is something to be reckoned with. Without meaning any harm, a Bloodhound can knock you down or pull you off your feet. If you have toddlers, small dogs, or are a small person with an unassuming personality, you need to consider how much dog you and your family can handle.

Messiness. Bloodhounds are messy. These are dogs whose fanciers have nicknamed them slobberhounds. They drool heavily and may well hold the world record for flinging slobber long distances. In "Lo, Hear the Gentle Bloodhound!" Thurber wrote, "He is a large, enormously evident creature, likely to make a housewife fear for her antiques and draperies." Will you mind following after this dog with a towel to wipe up wet spots or having your favorite outfit slimed just before you leave for work?

Odor. Bloodhounds have a distinctive odor. Some hounds, including this one, tend to have what is often described as a musty aroma. Like horse people who appreciate the smell of manure, hound people like the smell of their dogs; other people don't necessarily tolerate it as well. Take a good whiff before you decide to acquire a Bloodhound. Will you mind this smell permeating your house?

Character. Bloodhounds can be stubborn and dominant. If your only exposure to them has been Duke on reruns of "The Beverly Hillbillies," you are probably in for a surprise. Unlike Duke, who seemed to do nothing but laze around the house, most Blood-

hounds are moderately active dogs that like to be in control. For their entire history, they have been bred to be leaders, to forge ahead and find their prey without relying on human direction. These characteristics don't necessarily go along with being a good pet. Pleasing their owners is not what motivates Bloodhounds. They do things their way and have the size to back up their preference—unless they've been socialized and trained at an early age.

Exercise. Bloodhounds need a lot of daily exercise. They can follow a scent trail for miles. The longest trail ever followed by a Bloodhound was 138 miles (222 km). Relays of handlers were needed to keep up with the dog. Keeping a Bloodhound in good condition requires a serious commitment of time and effort, but the upside is that you'll be in good condition, too.

Advantages to Owning a Bloodhound

After reading all this, you may be wondering why anyone would want to own a Bloodhound. That's a good question, and it has several good answers. The most obvious, of course, is for its mantrailing powers. Bloodhounds are prized by police departments, search and rescue teams, and private owners who merely enjoy the sport of mantrailing and knowing that their dogs can help save a life if need be.

For the right family, a Bloodhound can make a wonderful companion. It's a breed that is large enough for roughhousing, yet gentle and tolerant of the antics of kids. Toddlers are easily knocked over by the exuberant Bloodhound, but older children will find them to be patient, active companions with a strong sense of humor.

Another reason for acquiring a Bloodhound is that it is a dog of great character with a strong sense of self. A description of the ideal Bloodhound was written in 1900 by Charles Henry

Many people find that Bloodhounds are addictive. It's hard to have just one.

Lane, who was an exhibitor and judge. In part, it read: "The hound strikes you as not over-large, but with great character, quality and much dignity. . . . The general appearance should be that of a high-classed, aristocratic and very dignified animal, who looks as if he considered himself fit company for emperors and would not care to associate with any except those belonging to the upper circles."

Despite its dominant disposition, the Bloodhound is a sensitive and reserved animal. For the experienced dog owner, a Bloodhound is an interesting and complicated companion. This owner has an understanding of and appreciation for the dog's differences and can provide the structure and leadership the Bloodhound needs to fit well into family life.

Owning a Bloodhound takes a high degree of commitment to the dog. If you believe you are ready to take that step, this book will help you find, train, and care for your Bloodhound and meet its special needs. And remember . . . like potato chips, it's hard to have just one. If one Bloodhound is good, two or more are even better!

Acquiring a Bloodhound Puppy

Choosing a Breeder

Finding the right source for your new puppy is the most important part of the buying process. A good breeder is hard to find and is a prize to be treasured once located. What makes a good breeder? Look for someone who is knowledgeable about and experienced in the breed, who loves the breed and wants only the best for it, and who gives his or her dogs top-notch care and training.

How can you identify this paragon? A good breeder has been involved in Bloodhounds—owning, showing, and breeding them—for at least five years. Length of time shows a commitment to the breed. Of course, someone who has been in the breed for less time can still be a good breeder, but ideally he or she is being guided by someone more experienced.

Why is it important that breeders show or work their Bloodhounds? A dog show is an opportunity for breeders to display the results of their breeding programs for evaluation by other breeders and judges. Breeders who work their dogs in search and rescue or in mantrailing trials are concerned about keeping the breed's historic working ability, which, of course, is dependent on sound physical and mental characteristics. Exhibiting or working a dog requires a commitment to a sound breeding program as well as to an individual dog's good health, grooming, and character. Breeders who show or work their Bloodhounds generally feed high-quality food,

ensure that their dogs have all the necessary vaccinations to protect them from disease, and socialize their pups by exposing them at an early age to all kinds of people, places, sounds, noises, and smells.

A good breeder tests breeding stock for genetic disorders before breeding so diseases won't be passed on to pups. Some of the hereditary conditions that affect Bloodhounds are ectropion, or loose eyelids; entropion, in which the eyelids roll inward; hip dysplasia; and elbow dysplasia, the most common form of which in the Bloodhound is ununited anconeal process (see page 76). Bloodhounds are also prone to hypertrophic osteodystrophy and fragmented coronoid process. Walk away from

Bloodhound puppies on the move, swirling through a world of scents.

breeders who say genetic testing is worthless or that their lines don't have any problems.

Whether a pup's parents have earned championships, know how to work a trail, or have been tested for genetic problems before being bred may not seem important to you if you are acquiring a Bloodhound solely as a companion, but it's financially smart to remember that your dog is a living being whose health and character rely on how well it has been raised. Wouldn't you rather buy a dog that has a head start in life through its parents' health and good qualities as well as its own good diet, vaccinations, worming, and early socialization than one raised without any thought for how it will eventually turn out?

To find a good breeder, start by writing to the national breed club (listed on page 92) for a list of recommended breeders. Be sure to enclose a self-addressed stamped envelope for the information, as well as when you write to a breeder. Even if the breeder you contact doesn't have puppies available, he or she may be able to refer you to someone else.

Note the following:

1. Whenever possible, visit the breeder's home and view the dogs' facilities. They should be clean and well kept. Avoid breeders who aren't willing to permit home visits or who offer to meet you on the freeway and sell you a puppy from their van. It may sound convenient, but it's likely that such a breeder isn't too concerned with any aspect of the dogs' well-being.

2. Be sure to meet the parents of the puppies. You can often judge a pup by its parents' appearance and temperaments. A shy or snappish mother is likely to pass on those traits to her pups. If one parent isn't available, ask to see photos or videos. Ask the age of the parents. Parents that are less than two years old are not yet fully mature, so avoid buying puppies produced by them.

3. When you buy, examine the contract closely. It should cover the rights of buyer and seller, any health guarantees, buy-back or return policies, spay/neuter requirements, and delivery of registration papers.

The Right Puppy

Once you've found a good breeder, the fun part begins: looking at and choosing from among the puppies. A Bloodhound puppy is a charming character, described by writer Richard Conniff as looking like a 39 short man in a 46 long suit. At eight weeks of age, it already shows promise not only of size but also of the breed's much celebrated curiosity. Bloodhound pups roll and tumble over each other and then race in all different directions, noses twitching to catch all the intriguing scents floating by.

Questions to Ask Breeders

- Do you belong to national and local Bloodhound clubs?
- How long have you been breeding Bloodhounds?
- Do you have any other breeds?
- How many litters have you bred?
- What are the most serious problems Bloodhounds have?
- What is it like to train a Bloodhound?
- What temperament problems might a Bloodhound have?
- What behavior problems can I expect?
- What type of contract, conditions, or guarantees are involved in the sale of the puppy?
- Can you give me references from other puppy buyers?

Beware the breeder who paints a glowing picture of life with a Bloodhound. No breed is perfect for everyone, least of all this one.

They all look cute, but your choice will be made easier once you decide whether you want a male or female, which color appeals to you, and whether you want to show the pup, use it in mantrailing, or just have it as a companion. In some instances, the breeder will make the decision for you, taking into account your preferences and lifestyle and his or her observations of the litter. Take the recommendation seriously; breeders have been watching their pups on a daily basis for at least eight weeks and are well aware of their personalities and aptitudes by this point.

When choosing a puppy, think about what you expect from your Bloodhound. If you want a companion, look for the puppy that comes running up to sniff you and then sticks around to be petted or held. If your goal is to take up mantrailing (see pages 57 to 60), your best choice may be the pup that is unusually confident and curious, one that always notices when people are around and comes over to investigate them. Always share your expectations with the breeder so he or she can help you make the right decision.

Male or Female?

Generally, there is no reason to prefer one sex over the other, except size. Males are usually at least 10 pounds (4.5 kg) larger and 2 inches (5.1 cm) taller than females. Both sexes are gentle and companionable, although either can dominate the household if given half a chance. Some mantrailing experts prefer females for their work, saying that they are less likely to be distracted on the trail.

Spaying/Neutering. Whatever sex you choose, if the Bloodhound is to be a pet it should be spayed or neutered before puberty, which usually occurs at six to nine months of age. Spaying or neutering a dog helps reduce prob-

Questions Breeders Will Ask You
- Why do you want a Bloodhound?
- What do you know about the breed?
- Have you owned a dog before and how long did it live?
- Do you own your own home?
- Do you have a fenced yard?
- What kind of shelter do you have for the dog when it's outside?
- How much time do you plan to spend with your Bloodhound?
- How will a Bloodhound fit into your lifestyle?
- Do you have children and how old are they?
- Will you spay or neuter a pet-quality dog?

lems with aggression and territorial urine-marking. Females who are spayed before their first heat have a much lower incidence of mammary tumors, uterine infections, and cancer of the uterus. Neutered males are less likely to display mounting behavior, have a decreased incidence of prostatic enlargement and neoplasia, and no longer run the risk of testicular tumors.

Large Litters

Because of their size, Bloodhounds have incredibly large litters, often of a dozen or more pups. Before you decide to breed your dog, ask yourself whether you have the time, energy, and money to deal with that many active, curious puppies. There is not a huge demand for Bloodhounds, so unless you have cash deposits in hand before you breed, it could take quite a while to place them all in suitable homes. The cost of spaying or neutering your Bloodhound is far less than that of breeding, raising, and placing a litter of puppies.

The long ears and wrinkles of a Bloodhound puppy are appealing, but there's a lot more to owning a Bloodhound than its cuteness.

A dog that has been sexually altered is much more likely to live a long and healthy life than one that is intact.

Buy your puppy from a breeder who keeps a clean kennel area and tests dogs for genetic defects before breeding. The puppies should look healthy and act friendly.

There's an old wives' tale that altered dogs get fat, but it's just that—a tale. What really happens is that the pup's metabolism starts to slow to its adult rate right around the time of puberty. Unless its diet and exercise level are adjusted, the dog will indeed gain weight, but not because of the spay/neuter surgery.

Which Color?

Bloodhounds come in three colors: black and tan, liver and tan, and red. The darker colors are sometimes interspersed with lighter or badger-colored hair, sometimes flecked with white. A small spot of white—which probably entered the gene pool from Foxhound crosses that took place to help bring the breed back after World War II—is allowed on the chest, feet, and the tip of the tail, but a blaze or socks would weigh heavily against a Bloodhound in the show ring or as a breeding prospect.

A Bloodhound's eye color is related to its coat color. Black-and-tan and red dogs tend to have hazel eyes, while liver-and-tan Bloodhounds are more likely to have yellow eyes. A deep hazel eye is preferred, no matter what the dog's coat color.

Papers

When you take your Bloodhound puppy home, the breeder will present you with an AKC application form, called a blue slip, that is filled out with the breed, sex, and color of the dog, the dog's date of birth, the registered names of the dog's sire and dam, and the breeder's name. To register the dog, simply complete the form with your name and address and the name you have chosen to register the dog under, and send it to the AKC with the proper fee. After the application is processed, you will be mailed an AKC registration certificate.

Some breeders withhold the registration form until the puppy has been spayed or neutered. Others use what is called a limited registration, meaning that your puppy can be registered, but none of its offspring can. Although dogs with limited registration cannot be shown in conformation, they can take part in American Bloodhound Club mantrailing trials and AKC performance events such as obedience, agility, and tracking. Breeders often use the limited registration when they are not sure of a pup's potential as a show or breeding animal. If the pup grows up to be a quality dog, and you and the breeder both agree it should be bred, the breeder can then change the limited registration to full registration.

The breeder may also give you a copy of your Bloodhound's pedigree, which is a written record of the dog's ancestry for three generations or more. A pedigree has no legal standing, but it contains important information if you intend to breed your dog.

Other paperwork the breeder should provide includes the pup's veterinary records, indicating which vaccinations it has received and when, whether it has been dewormed, and results of any tests for hereditary disorders. A careful breeder will also give you a packet of information regarding the food your puppy has been eating, how often it is used to being fed, and other advice that will help the two of you make a smooth adjustment to living together.

Naming Your Puppy

When choosing a name for a Bloodhound, your options are many. For instance, you can focus on the breed's reputation as a crime solver, selecting a name from among the many fictional detectives lurking in literature and television, or even the creators of those detectives. Good names include Columbo, Marlowe, Sherlock, McGee, Poirot, The Saint, Agatha, and Edgar

(Mr. Poe is famous as the creator of the first murder mystery). Poirot is especially apt since the little detective with the mustache is from Belgium, the traditional home of the Bloodhound; The Saint makes reference not only to the literary and film character but also to the breed's originator, St. Hubert.

Despite its troubles there, the Bloodhound also has a strong association with the Deep South. If you're a fan of

These two dogs show the difference in size between puppy and adult Bloodhounds.

Acquiring an Adult Bloodhound

Not everyone can adjust to life with a Bloodhound. Each year, several hundred Bloodhounds nationwide are turned in to Bloodhound rescue groups, which must then find good homes for them; other Bloodhounds end up in animal shelters. If you can give a Bloodhound a good home and don't mind going home with an adolescent or adult dog, adopting one from a rescue group may be a good way to go. Be sure to discuss thoroughly with rescue personnel why the dog was given up, to ensure that you will be able to provide the dog with a suitable environment and behavioral structure. To find a Bloodhound rescue group, see the listing on page 92.

Gone With the Wind or have an interest in the Civil War, some names you might consider are Rhett, Scarlett, Colonel, Tara, Margaret, Mitchell, and Dixie.

Of course, there are also names relating to the Bloodhound's physical and behavioral characteristics, such as Droopy, Snooper, and Tracker. And since the French and the Celts were famed for their fine hounds, try searching baby name books for French or Celtic names that you like.

Some possibilities are Belle; Duke, an Old French word meaning leader, which is a fitting choice for a dog that is always out in front; Mungo, a Celtic word meaning lovable; or Meara, the Gaelic word for mirth, which is perfectly appropriate, given the Bloodhound's sense of humor. The most common Bloodhound names are Buford, Rufus, Beauregard, Wrinkles, and Duke for males, Ruby, Daisy, Daisy-Mae, and Annabel for females.

Puppy Care

Bloodhound Essentials: What to Get before You Bring Your Puppy Home

The key to living successfully with a Bloodhound is preparation. Knowing what to expect from your new dog and being ready for any contingency puts you at the head of the puppy-owner pack. This readiness extends even to such details as putting together a puppy layette before you pick up your new family member from the breeder. Before the big day arrives, purchase a collar, identification tag, leash, food, feeding dishes, crate, and toys. Your foresight will help your puppy feel at home more quickly and will help you adjust as well.

Collar and Tag

Before setting off on your shopping spree, call the breeder and ask a few questions. What size collar does your pup need? Is nylon or leather recommended? Usually, nylon is preferred for its durability, light weight, and low cost. Whether you choose nylon or leather, the collar should always be a flat buckle style, not a choke-type training collar. A choke collar should be worn only when the dog is being trained and is under supervision. It's very easy for this type of collar to get hung up on something and choke the dog. A buckle collar can be adjusted as your puppy grows. You should always be able to fit two fingers between the collar and the pup's neck.

Order an engraved identification tag, even if you don't know what your pup's name will be yet. The tag should have your name, address, and phone number on it. Put the collar and tag on the pup before you walk out of the breeder's house. A nylon or leather leash will help you keep the puppy under control in its new surroundings.

Food

Another question to ask the breeder is what the puppy has been eating and buy a supply of that food, even if you don't plan to continue feeding it. Switching a puppy to a new diet too quickly can cause diarrhea. Gradually mix small amounts of the new food into the old food so the pup's digestive system has time to adjust. Whatever food you choose, be sure it is labeled complete and balanced, with high-quality ingredients, and is formulated for puppy growth. Diet is one area where you don't want to skimp on your Bloodhound's care.

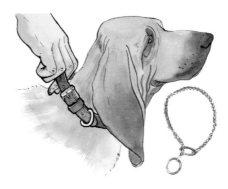

A buckle collar is for everyday wear, while a choke collar should be used only during training sessions. Always remove a choke collar if you can't be there to supervise.

Feeding Dishes

Of course, you'll also need a set of food and water dishes. Ideally, your Bloodhound will eat from raised dishes to help prevent bloat or gastric torsion (see page 75); most such dishes are made of metal. Metal dishes are recommended because they can withstand being batted around and chewed on by a puppy, and they're easy to clean. Plastic dishes can be chewed up and swallowed by your Bloodhound, causing an obstruction, so it's best not to use them.

A Crate

A crate is one of the most important purchases you will make. It allows your puppy to ride safely in the car, gives the pup a place where it can feel secure, and is a super housetraining tool (see page 27). The crate can be made of wire or plastic, depending on your needs. A wire crate offers better ventilation and folds up for storage, but a plastic crate is the best choice if your dog will be traveling frequently by air.

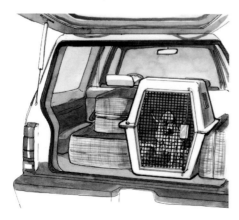

A crate is useful for housetraining as well as for travel.

Toys

Last, but not least, be sure to buy a couple of toys to keep your Bloodhound entertained and out of trouble. A good chew toy will distract your puppy from chewing on things it shouldn't. Choose toys that are sturdy, with no buttons or bells that can be chewed off and swallowed. Favorite Bloodhound toys are large rawhides, sterile bones, Nylabones, and rope bones. Any toy you give your Bloodhound should be something large that it can't chew up easily.

Once your purchases are made, the only thing remaining to be done is to pick up your pup. Then begins the wildest ride of your life: Bloodhound puppyhood. Having a Bloodhound puppy around the house is absolute mayhem, so being prepared is essential for your sanity.

First Days Home: Puppy-Proofing the House and Yard

With any puppy it's important to make the home environment a safe place to be, but a Bloodhound puppy is a special challenge. With 1,200 years of genetic selection for sniffing ability behind it, nothing is safe from a curious Bloodhound. These dogs love to chew and dig, and they have a strong ability to focus on whatever they're doing. They will eat patio furniture, and a number of them have even been known to chew the wiring out of cars. Intestinal obstructions are common in Bloodhounds. Items that are especially likely to cause problems include:

- bones
- corn cobs
- peach pits
- children's toys
- fishing line
- foil and plastic wrap
- pantyhose and underwear
- rocks
- small balls and sponges

With this in mind, take extra-special care to puppy-proof your home and yard:

1. Use child safety locks on kitchen and bathroom cabinets that contain cleansers and medications.

2. Keep garbage out of reach or in an area that is off limits to your puppy. Using a trash compactor is even better, as long as you are careful to always keep its door closed.

3. Wrap up electrical cords so they are less noticeable to a pup's roving eye, and coat cords with Bitter Apple or some other nasty substance that will deter them from chewing.

4. Put rat bait or other poisonous substances such as antifreeze in locked cabinets in the garage. For even greater safety, buy antifreeze that contains the less toxic propylene glycol rather than ethylene glycol.

5. Take note of your house plants and landscaping as well. Many common house and yard plants are toxic to dogs. These include caladium, dieffenbachia or dumb cane, elephant's ear, and philodendron. Other plants that have toxic properties include bulbs such as amaryllis, daffodils, hyacinth, iris, jonquils, narcissus, azaleas, English ivy, holly berries, hydrangea, jasmine, ligustrum and privet hedges, oleander, and wisteria. If you have any of these plants, put them out of the dog's reach, isolate them with some type of barrier, or build a run for your dog in a safe area of the yard.

Never assume that your Bloodhound can't or won't get into something. Get down on your hands and knees and explore your house at puppy level to make sure you haven't missed any potential dangers.

Feeding Your Puppy

Bloodhound puppies grow at a dramatic rate, but it's important not to push their growth. Bigger is not better.

Be sure to puppy-proof your house or apartment before you bring your new arrival home.

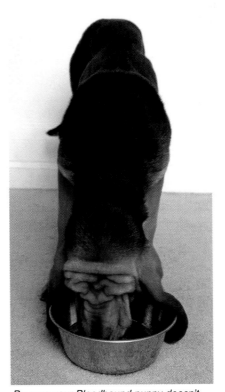

Be sure your Bloodhound puppy doesn't overeat. Rapid growth can lead to problems with bone and joint development.

If your Bloodhound grows too quickly or puts on too much weight, bone and joint problems can result. For the same reason, you should avoid giving calcium supplements.

Discuss the best food for your pup with your veterinarian, and take the pup in regularly to be weighed. (Most veterinarians don't charge fees just for weighing the dog.) Bloodhound puppies usually eat three to four times daily until they are six to nine months old. Start cutting meals back when your dog shows less interest in the midday meal.

Dogs like a routine. Your Bloodhound will do best when you feed it at the same time and the same place every day. Feed your dog in a quiet place where there isn't a lot of coming and going, and wait to feed it if it has been exerting itself. Avoid switching foods frequently. Sudden changes in diet can cause intestinal upset, and your dog may also develop picky eating habits.

After your Bloodhound finishes eating, thoroughly clean the flews (lips) and dewlap (the loose skin that hangs beneath the throat and neck). You may even want to use a snood to keep the ears out of the food. Put your Bloodhound in its crate to rest after it eats. Heavy exercise and drinking too much water after eating are frequently linked to gastric torsion, a potentially fatal condition (see page 75).

Outdoor Shelter and Confinement

When your Bloodhound is outside, a good, sturdy doghouse is a must to protect it from the elements. Doghouses come in many shapes and styles, and can be made of wood or plastic. With the Bloodhound's propensity for chewing, plastic may be the better choice. The doghouse should be large enough for the dog to stand up, turn around, and lie down comfortably. Place it in an area that offers plenty of shade. Ideally, it will face south or east for protection from cold north winds.

If possible, provide your Bloodhound with a pen or run in the yard. That way, you can keep it safe from any poisonous plants and confine digging to a specific area. A good size is 10 feet by 30 feet (3 m x 9 m) or larger. Gravel is the best ground cover for a Bloodhound's pen. It's good for the dog's feet, and it's small enough to pass through the digestive tract if swallowed.

A fenced yard is a must for a Bloodhound. With that inquisitive nose always twitching, this is not a breed that can ever be permitted to run loose. Bloodhounds do not have a homing instinct; their talent lies in following a trail, not in backtracking. Be sure your yard or the dog's pen is surrounded by a sturdy fence with a gate that latches automatically. A 6-foot (1.8 m) chain link fence is ideal. Otherwise, look for loose boards or areas where a hole could be dug to facilitate escape and repair them. To keep your Bloodhound from digging under the fence, you may need skirts beneath

Your puppy needs tough chew toys that it can't shred and swallow, and an enclosed outdoor area for its safety as well as the safety of your yard and garden.

the fence that spread out underground. Some Bloodhounds are climbers or jumpers. An electric wire across the top of the fence will help to discourage them. Don't think that an underground electronic fence will be enough to contain your Bloodhound. When a scent attracts them, Bloodhounds are so highly motivated to follow it that the shock delivered by the system won't deter them.

Housetraining

Bloodhounds are very clean dogs and they are easily housetrained. However, they are not mature enough to hold their bladder until they are four to six months old, so trustworthy housetraining is not possible until then. Despite this, you should begin housetraining as early as eight weeks of age, when memory truly begins in the puppy. This will deeply imprint the training in the pup's psyche.

As with any type of training, consistency is the key. Take your pup out several times a day to eliminate. This elimination schedule should take place as nearly as possible at the same time each day. A typical schedule might be first thing in the morning after waking, immediately after each meal, and just before bedtime.

Always take your puppy out on leash to eliminate. This accomplishes two things: It allows you to be sure the pup has urinated and defecated, and it helps the puppy form an association between going out and eliminating. Praise your puppy as it eliminates. Again, this creates pleasant associations for the pup. After the pup has done its business, take it right back inside so it will strongly associate the outdoors with elimination, then place it in its crate to rest.

How does a crate serve as a housetraining tool? Dogs are den animals, and they are conditioned not to soil their den, or sleeping, areas. By putting the puppy in the crate when you can't supervise it, you prevent accidents in the house. This is good for you, because you don't have to clean them up, and good for the pup, because it doesn't get scolded for making a mistake. Whenever possible, you should make sure your Bloodhound only has opportunities to do the right thing. That will make life easier for both of you.

Confinement in the House

A crate is also useful for keeping a puppy out of harm's way and protecting your clothes, shoes, furniture, and other household items from sharp puppy teeth. Make it a habit to put your puppy in the crate whenever you can't keep an eye on it. The crate is not a place of punishment; rather, it's a place of rest where your pup can't get into trouble and won't be bothered by inquisitive children or other pets.

The idea, however, is not to isolate your Bloodhound. Keep the crate in an area where there's plenty of family activity, such as the den or kitchen. Remind children that the crate is off limits when the puppy is inside—no banging on the top or poking fingers inside.

At night, the puppy can sleep in its crate in your bedroom. Your presence will be reassuring, especially to a pack animal like the Bloodhound. Also, you'll be right there to take the puppy out when you first hear it stirring in the morning.

Except overnight or on a plane flight, never leave your puppy or adult dog in a crate for more than four hours at a time. A puppy can't control its bladder for much longer than that, and no dog should be kept confined for long periods without companionship or exercise.

You can also use a wire mesh baby gate or exercise pen to confine your dog to an area such as the kitchen, bathroom, or laundry room. There's a

Leash Training

Bloodhounds are curious and will eat or dig up just about anything. Puppy-proof your home and yard carefully.

little more room for your dog to explore, and the tile or linoleum floors are easy to clean if it has an accident. Of course, you'll want to make sure the room is puppy-proofed first.

With patient, consistent training, a Bloodhound can learn to walk nicely on a leash without pulling too much.

On-leash activity is the only safe way for your Bloodhound to exercise in an open area. Bloodhounds have no car sense, or indeed any sense of what's around them other than what they're interested in at the moment. We know of one Bloodhound following a trail on railroad tracks that was killed when she paid no attention to an oncoming train.

Walking a Bloodhound on leash is an experience. Bloodhound fancier Roger Caras says that Bloodhound people always seem to have one arm that is a little longer than the other. It is possible, however, to teach your dog to walk nicely on leash. The key is to begin early and practice often. You have only a small window of opportunity before your Bloodhound weighs as much as or more than you do.

Accustom your puppy to the leash from day one. Let the pup wear the leash around the house, dragging the leash behind it. Your puppy may twist and turn, trying to rid itself of the strange new "tail," but that's perfectly normal. Let the pup get used to the leash at its own pace. When it stops fighting with the leash, call it and reward it with praise and a treat if it comes to you. The intent is for the puppy to associate wearing the leash with good things.

The next step is to encourage the puppy to follow you while you're holding the leash. Hold it loose and low, and call the puppy as you walk forward. Again, give praise and a treat if the pup complies. Practice walking with the leash for a few minutes several times a day, and always make it fun. Stop before the puppy gets bored or frustrated. In puppy kindergarten, your Bloodhound will get more practice in walking on a leash.

Trainer Brian Kilcommons emphasizes the importance of letting your dog "ask questions" about leash training. Keep the leash loose so the puppy can experiment with what's allowed and what's not. If the pup pulls, correct it. Praise it when it walks nicely without pulling.

Bloodhounds do love to pull, and it's not something that is easily trained out of them (nor should it be if you plan to use yours for mantrailing). A good compromise might be to use a retractable leash, which allows your dog to range out to 16 feet (4.9 cm). If this is not an option, try using a head collar to keep pulling to a minimum. A head collar resembles a horse halter and works on the principle that by controlling the head, you control the rest of the body. Used correctly, it is a safe, gentle method of keeping your dog under control.

Don't use a harness for your Bloodhound unless you're using it for mantrailing. A harness offers no control and will only encourage the dog to pull more. Instead, use a training collar (nylon or metal choke collar) or a head collar. Don't use the regular flat collar because it's likely to slip off if the dog pulls hard enough.

Riding in the Car

It's always an advantage to have a dog that rides well in the car. Trips to the veterinarian go much easier when the dog isn't throwing itself all around the car or loudly throwing up in the backseat. And for a show or mantrailing Bloodhound, frequent car travel is essential. So are good car manners.

The polite Bloodhound respects your authority and learns to wait until you give the okay before jumping in or out of the car. For greatest safety, your dog should ride in a crate or be confined by a harness that attaches to the seatbelt. If you have to stop suddenly, you don't want 100 pounds (45 kg) of Bloodhound flying through the windshield!

To accustom your dog to riding in the car, take it on brief errands to the bank or post office. If it's lucky, the drive-up bank teller will give it a biscuit. As with any other type of training, praise the dog for riding nicely and correct it when it misbehaves. Howling along with you to the music on the radio is okay; non-stop barking or hanging its head out the window aren't.

This Bloodhound is eagerly awaiting an invitation to ride in the car.

Take your Bloodhound on brief errands to accustom it to riding in the car or truck.

29

HOW-TO:
Teaching Good Manners

If a puppy class isn't available in your area, you can still teach proper canine etiquette to your Bloodhound at home. Besides leash training, a puppy needs to know the commands for *sit, down, stay,* and *come.* They are the foundation of a well-trained dog that you can take anywhere.

Don't force your pup into the down *position. Gentle persuasion works better, especially with this somewhat stubborn breed.*

Sit

Sit is one of the easiest commands to teach. Get your puppy's attention, show it a treat, and then raise the treat directly above its head. The puppy will naturally move into a sitting position. When it does, say "*Sit*" and give the treat. Practice this for a couple of minutes several times a day. Your dog will soon associate the word *sit* with the action of sitting (and receiving a treat). Once the puppy is sitting consistently on command, scale back the treats to every other sit, and then to every three or four sits. Eventually, you can phase out the treats and offer praise instead.

Down

Once your pup has learned to *sit,* you can introduce the command for *down.* This time, as your pup is sitting, show a treat and move it downward and forward until it is in front of the puppy's paws. The puppy should move naturally into the *down* position. When it does, say "*Down*" and reward it with the treat. Practice this the same way you did for the *sit* command.

The trick with these first two commands is not to confuse your dog. Use only the words "*Sit*" and "*Down.*" Don't tell your dog to "*Sit down*" or "*Lie down*" or it won't know what you're talking about. For the same reason, if the dog jumps up on you or on a forbidden piece of furniture, say "*Off,*" not "*Down.*"

Stay

Next, teach your puppy to stay in a sitting or *down* position. It's probably easiest to start with the *down* position. Put a leash on the dog so you can control its actions. Standing in front of it, lean over, say "*Down,*" then put your hand, palm forward, in front of its face and say "*Stay.*" Stand up and step back a few paces. Don't rush, and don't go too slowly. Remain there for only a few seconds and return to the dog. As you do, put your foot on the leash so the pup can't get up. Praise the pup for staying, and then give a release command such as "*Okay*" to indicate that it can get up.

If your dog gets up after you've told it to stay, simply

Lure your puppy into a sitting position by raising your hand up over its head, causing the pup's head to go up and its rear down. A treat in your hand will add further interest if necessary.

place it back in the *down* position without scolding and start over. You may have to settle for one- or two-second *stays* at first. Patience is a must.

Gradually increase the distance you go and length of time you stay. Aim for a 10-minute *stay,* and take plenty of time to get there. Always give lots of praise before releasing the dog from the *stay*. Once your dog has learned to *stay* while lying down, you can link the *stay* and *sit* commands.

Every good-mannered pup learns to heed the "Stay!" command.

Come

The most important command any dog can know is the one for *"come,"* but it's difficult to teach to a hound. Make the act of coming to you as pleasant and enticing as possible. Rattle a box of treats to get your dog's attention and say, *"Sherlock, come!"* Use a happy, excited tone of voice. When he responds, heap on the praise and treats.

Once you've established that coming to your call is well worth the effort, teaching this command can take a more formal turn. Attach a 20- to 30-foot (6.1–9 m) clothesline to Sherlock's collar and start running away from him, feeding out the line as you go. Don't let it get tight. When you get a good distance away, call him to you. If he responds, keep backing away while encouraging him to follow you. If he doesn't respond, use the line to draw him toward you,

still praising him for coming. Use this technique only once per training session. Save a repeat for another day.

Never use the *come* command to call your dog for something unpleasant such as a scolding or being given a pill.

That's the quickest way to teach a dog *not* to come.

Puppies, and especially Bloodhounds, have brief attention spans, so keep training sessions short, and always end them when your dog has been successful, not after a correction.

Teach the "Come!" command first on a leash, then later off lead. Always be welcoming when you want your Bloodhound to come to you. Never call it for anything unpleasant such as a scolding or a bath.

Puppy Kindergarten

Forget you ever heard that old wives' tale about waiting until a dog is six months old to train it. By that time, your Bloodhound will be huge and well on its way to running the household. Early training in puppy kindergarten, beginning when the pup is nine to twelve weeks old, is highly recommended. Your breeder may be able to refer you to a class run by the local dog club, or one may be offered by your veterinarian.

The good manners your puppy will learn in kindergarten include the commands for *sit, stay, down,* and *come*. The pup will also learn to walk nicely on a leash and accept handling for grooming and veterinary exams. You will learn the basics of housetraining and problem prevention, the best ways to motivate your puppy, and how to time rewards and corrections so they have an effect. Socialization is another aspect of puppy kindergarten. Your Bloodhound will meet lots of new dogs and people there, and you'll play fun games like "Pass the Puppy," so all the dogs become accustomed to being petted and handled by other people.

Before you start a class, ask the trainer which breeds he or she has had experience with. Golden retrievers are a lot easier and quicker to train than Bloodhounds, and you and your dog may require special attention and effort from the trainer. No matter what the breed, the good puppy trainer uses only positive training methods and is never rough or harsh with students, whether they are canine or human.

A puppy kindergarten class can also help you spot problems in the making. The trainer may identify possessive or territorial traits in your dog that you hadn't recognized. Getting professional help at this early stage can give your dog a needed attitude adjustment before it's too big to control.

Visiting the Veterinarian

Your Bloodhound's first visit to the veterinarian should be a positive experience. The pup will receive a thorough physical exam and any

Vaccination Chart

Vaccine	Age
Distemper/measles/parainfluenza	6 to 8 weeks
Parvovirus	6 to 8 weeks
Distemper, hepatitis, leptospirosis, parainfluenza, parvovirus (DHLPP)	8 to 12 weeks
Coronavirus (optional)	12 weeks
Coronavirus (optional)	16 weeks
DHLPP	16 weeks
Rabies	16 weeks
Parvovirus (optional)	18 to 20 weeks
DHLPP	Annually after puppy series is completed
Coronavirus (optional)	Annually after puppy series is completed
Rabies	1 year, triannually thereafter*

*In some states, a rabies vaccination is required annually. Your veterinarian can advise you.

booster vaccinations it needs to fight off the infectious diseases that threaten dogs: parvovirus, distemper, hepatitis, leptospirosis, and parainfluenza. Depending on your veterinarian's recommendation, your puppy may also be vaccinated for coronavirus, canine cough, and Lyme disease. At four months of age, your Bloodhound will need to be vaccinated against rabies.

A fecal exam is also a good idea. Bring a fresh stool sample so the veterinarian can examine it for signs of internal parasites such as roundworms, tapeworms, hookworms, and whipworms, and treat your puppy if needed.

While the veterinarian examines your puppy, take this opportunity to ask for advice on dental care, grooming (especially nail trimming), nutrition, and spaying and neutering. You might also ask the veterinarian to explain emergency or first aid procedures in case your Bloodhound swallows and chokes on an object or eats something poisonous. Be sure you know what number to call for after-hours emergencies and where the nearest emergency clinic is located. Because Bloodhounds are so rare, this may be your veterinarian's first experience with one. It's to be hoped that he or she won't have any misconceptions about the breed's temperament, but if that's the case, your pup will no doubt quickly put them to rest with its irresistible manner.

Bloodhounds and Other Pets

Bloodhounds are friendly and get along well with other dogs and cats. Your cat may object to being drooled on by your Bloodhound, but that is likely to be the only problem you encounter with the two. Of course, you'll need to be careful about the interactions you permit if your other dog is a small, fragile breed such as

If you live or travel in an area where there are ticks, ask your veterinarian about Lyme disease vaccine.

an Italian Greyhound or Chihuahua. Without meaning any harm, your Bloodhound could injure such a small dog by playing too roughly or accidentally stepping on it. Like most dogs, Bloodhounds recognize their own kind and especially enjoy being around others of their breed.

Good Dog Owner, Good Neighbor

When you bring a dog into your life, the decision affects more than just you and the dog. It affects everyone you and your Bloodhound come in contact with, especially your neighbors, who will most likely encounter your dog on a daily basis. You can ensure a happy relationship among all concerned by teaching your dog good manners and practicing responsible pet ownership. This includes training your dog so that it doesn't jump up on people or bark excessively, walking your dog on leash so that it doesn't run wild throughout the neighborhood, providing proper confinement, and picking up waste so that it doesn't attract flies and vermin or foul your neighbors' lawns.

Teaching your Bloodhound proper behavior when it's young is perhaps the most important thing you can do, both for your own enjoyment of the dog's companionship as well as for your neighbors' pleasure and peace of mind. If you've ever lived near someone who had an unruly dog, you know how annoying it can be: kids and garbage cans being knocked down, and barking at all hours of the day and night.

To keep the peace and prevent problems from ever starting, be sure your dog is under control—preferably on leash—when other people are around, and avoid situations that might cause your dog to bark unceasingly. These include frequently being left alone for long periods or left without any means of entertainment, such as toys. Fortunately, Bloodhounds are not known for being barkers, but their voices are deep and loud. When they do bark, everyone knows it. If your neighbors complain, keep an open, understanding mind, and try to determine the cause of the barking. People will be more patient if they see that you are honestly trying to solve the problem. Training techniques for dogs that jump up or bark too much are covered in the chapter on training, beginning on page 43.

Keeping your Bloodhound properly confined is another important aspect of owning this breed. The poet Robert Frost wrote that good fences make good neighbors, and this is especially true for the Bloodhound owner. Its powerful nose is constantly urging it to explore far beyond the boundaries of its yard or kennel. A good fence will keep your Bloodhound from trampling flower gardens, checking out the trash, and any number of other canine misdemeanors.

Picking up waste is probably everyone's least favorite aspect of dog ownership, but it's also one of the most important. Feces spread disease, attract flies and other vermin, smell bad, and are disgusting to step in. Ideally, you should teach your dog to eliminate in a specific spot in your yard, and then keep the area clean. If your dog does make a deposit on someone else's lawn, be prepared with a poop scoop or plastic bag to pick it up and take it home for disposal. Try to keep your dog from urinating on other lawns as well. Dog urine is acidic and can burn lawns, leaving unsightly yellow spots. Your neighbors will appreciate your thoughtfulness.

Bloodhound Maintenance

Coat Care

Grooming a Bloodhound is pretty simple. Its short coat is easy to brush, and the only other work needed is regular nail trimming, ear cleaning, and mouth care. Bathing is necessary only when the dog is dirty. Don't think that a bath will help reduce that houndy odor. The odor is built in, and a bath won't make it go away.

Start accustoming your puppy to being groomed as soon as you take it home. Even a squirmy Bloodhound can learn to sit still for a few minutes while being brushed and having its eyes and ears cleaned. This will make it easier for you and other people to handle the dog, something that's especially important for trips to the veterinarian's office or being judged at shows.

Save your back. Grooming will be easiest if your dog is up on a grooming table, picnic bench, or other flat, sturdy surface. Since your Bloodhound will grow quickly, one of the first things it should learn is how to jump up on the table. Encourage your dog to jump up by patting the table and saying "*Table*." Praise it or give a treat when it complies.

Brushing

Regular brushing is the foundation of the grooming process. Using a rubber hound glove, which can be purchased at a pet supply store, brush your Bloodhound weekly or even daily. Brushing removes loose hair and dead skin cells, distributes skin oils, and helps keep the coat shiny. It feels good, too, and your dog will soon come to enjoy being brushed. Avoid brushes with long or sharp bristles, such as pin brushes or wire slicker brushes. During the shedding season, a terrier stripping blade can come in handy to remove loose coat.

Vacuuming

Another good way to keep a Bloodhound clean is with a vacuum hose. Yes, some Bloodhounds enjoy being vacuumed. Vacuuming pulls out loose hair, dirt and dust in the coat, and fleas and flea eggs. Combined with brushing, vacuuming can keep your Bloodhound very clean. To accustom your puppy to the sound of the vacuum, let it hear and see it first. Bring

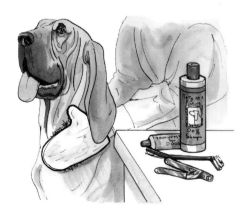

Grooming tools you'll need include a rubber hound glove, shampoo, nail trimmers, and a toothbrush.

Brush your Bloodhound regularly to keep its skin and coat healthy.

the hose (no attachments) up to the pup slowly so you don't frighten it, and gently move it over the dog's entire body. Like brushing, vacuuming feels good, so your dog should enjoy it if introduced properly.

A well-groomed Bloodhound shines with good health.

Bathing

It's rare that a Bloodhound needs a bath. Only if your dog is exceptionally dirty or is competing in a show should it need one. That's good, because by the time you and the dog are finished with the bath, you may need to redecorate the bathroom! There will be lots of shaking of wet dog going on, so wear old clothes that you don't mind getting wet, and pull together your supplies before you bring the dog in. You'll need plenty of towels, cotton balls to place in the ears to keep the water out, and a shampoo made for dogs. Put a drop of mineral oil in each eye to help keep water out. Wet the dog thoroughly with warm water, and lather, starting at the head and working your way to the tail. Rinse well, being sure to get all the shampoo out from under the folds of skin. Leftover soap on the skin can be irritating. A vinegar rinse (one part cider vinegar to one part water) can help ensure that you get all the soap out of the coat. Blot up as much water from the coat as possible and towel-dry the dog thoroughly. Don't let the dog outside or in any cold or drafty areas until it's completely dry. (This is a good time for the dog to be in its crate.) Put a sweatshirt on the dog or wrap a blanket around it to keep it warm while it dries. Consider using a forced-air dryer to get the dog completely dry in a timely manner.

Coat and Skin Problems

Itching, coat loss, and hot spots can have a number of causes, from external parasites such as fleas and mites to allergies to deficiencies caused by poor nutrition. It's pretty easy to determine whether a Bloodhound has fleas, but other skin problems will probably require a little detective work to identify and treat. For instance, a food allergy requires switching the dog to a food containing ingredients the dog has never eaten before. For a trial period of six to eight weeks, the dog must eat only this food—no treats, rawhides, or table scraps. At the end of the trial period, you can see whether the dog's skin condition has improved. If it has, the next step is to add ingredients back into the dog's diet, one at a time, to figure out what's causing the allergic response. Once that is determined, the dog can be placed on a diet that doesn't contain the offending ingredient.

Non-food allergies can be caused by pollen, cats, certain grasses or molds, or such things as chemicals in carpets. Allergy tests are available from veterinary dermatologists, who can then put your dog on a desensitization program. Allergy shots may be necessary to keep the condition under control. Fortunately, allergies are not especially common in Bloodhounds.

If a nutritional deficiency is suspected, your veterinarian will probably recommend switching the dog to a higher quality food that is complete and balanced for the dog's life stage. For instance, a young puppy being fed a food for adult dogs may not be getting enough protein and fat in its diet. Dogs that eat primarily table scraps can also lack proper nutrition.

Other conditions that can affect your dog's skin are ringworm, seborrhea, and thyroid deficiency. Your veterinarian can diagnose these problems and suggest an appropriate course of treatment. To learn more about the problems caused by fleas and mites, see pages 84 and 87.

Dental Care

To keep its mouth healthy, clean out your Bloodhound's flews after every meal, and brush its teeth. Brushing prevents the formation of plaque and tartar, and keeps bacteria from multiplying and causing infection. For best results, brushing should be done daily, but even a weekly brushing is better

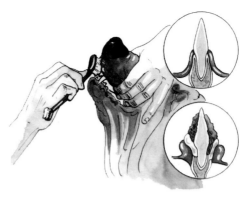

Brush your Bloodhound's teeth once a week to prevent development of plaque and tartar.

than nothing. Use a soft toothbrush and a toothpaste made for dogs (toothpaste made for humans can cause stomach upset in dogs). You

To help prevent infections, keep your Bloodhound's ears clean and dry.

37

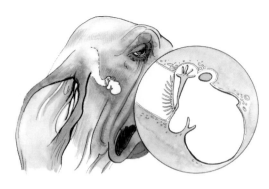

Anatomy of the ear.

can also make your own toothpaste by making a paste of baking soda, a little salt, and water. To help keep tartar scraped off between brushings, feed hard biscuits or dry food, and make sure your dog has access to dentally beneficial toys such as rope bones or rawhides.

Eyes and Ears

Keep the corners of the eyes free of dried mucus, and the ears dry and

Clip nails just before they curve so you won't hit the quick.

clean. One way to do this is to wipe the ears out with witch hazel every week. Keep an eye out for ear mites or signs of ear infection, such as redness, tenderness, or the dog shaking its head frequently or pawing at its ears (see page 89 for more about treatment of ear mites).

Anal Sacs

At the other end of your Bloodhound are its anal sacs, the contents of which serve to lubricate and mark your dog's feces as they are eliminated. The anal sacs are internal, but you can feel them externally on each side of the anus. Anal sacs sometimes become impacted, causing the dog to lick at its rear or scoot it across the floor or ground in an attempt to release the contents. Check the anal sacs regularly to make sure they aren't impacted. Your veterinarian can show you how to empty the anal sacs if necessary.

Nail Care

Most important, keep the nails well trimmed. Bloodhounds are sensitive about their feet, and yours will probably act as if you are killing it when you trim the nails, but don't let it fool you. When done properly and often, nail trimming doesn't hurt and is an important part of keeping the dog's feet healthy. Use a large nail trimmer made for dogs and clip just at the curve of the nail. If the nails are light-colored or clear, you can see the dark line of the quick. Avoid nicking it, because that is painful and can cause the nail to bleed. Keep some Quik-Stop or cornstarch handy to stop the bleeding if you make a mistake. The breeder or your veterinarian can show you where to trim to avoid any problems.

Nutrition

Choosing a Food

Food is the fuel that keeps the Bloodhound's body operating. The components of food are protein, fat, carbohydrates, vitamins, and minerals. Protein, which is made up of smaller units called amino acids, builds strong muscles and connective tissue such as hair, skin, cartilage, ligaments, and tendons, and it's critical for an effective immune system. Fat cushions the vital organs and is a highly digestible source of energy. Carbohydrates also provide energy, as well as fiber for proper function of the gastrointestinal tract, and they are essential in the formation of certain amino acids and other body compounds and tissues. Vitamins and minerals, although they are present only in tiny amounts, are needed by the body to carry out a number of metabolic processes.

It's clear, then, that choosing the right food can profoundly affect a Bloodhound's well-being. A diet that is complete and balanced provides just the right mix of all these substances to meet a dog's needs. Pet food formulation is governed by the American Association of Feed Control Officials, which decides the minimum and maximum requirements for a food to be labeled nutritionally adequate. Manufacturers of pet food spend millions of dollars each year studying the nutritional needs of dogs and developing and testing formulas.

The most effective way of testing a food is through feeding trials, in which a number of dogs are fed the diet over an extended period. Researchers make careful observations about the dogs' physical response to the food—overall health, coat condition, type and amount of feces produced—and whether the dogs like the food. After all, a food can't do much good if a dog won't eat it.

Reading Labels

Manufacturers are also permitted to test a food's nutritional value through chemical analysis, but this is a much less precise method than feeding trials. The label is required to state how a food's nutritional value was determined, and you are better off selecting one whose claims include the terms "complete and balanced," "feeding tests," "AAFCO feeding test protocols," or "AAFCO feeding studies."

The label will also indicate the life stage for which the food is formulated, such as puppies, adults, or aging dogs. Dogs have different nutritional needs at different times in their lives. Your veterinarian and the breeder can advise you on when to switch your Bloodhound from a puppy food to an adult maintenance food, but generally six months is a good age at which to make this change.

Ingredients

As you evaluate foods, be sure you understand how to read an ingredient list. Ingredients are listed by weight, in decreasing order. In other words, if chicken is the first ingredient listed, there is more chicken in the food than any other ingredient. Sometimes, different forms of the same ingredient are listed separately—for instance, ground rice, rice flour, and rice bran—so there may be more of a certain

The prepared Bloodhound owner always has a drool towel handy to wipe flews and dewlaps.

ingredient than it appears at first glance. Take these "split ingredients" into account when you're evaluating the makeup of a food.

Ideally, a food will contain high-quality sources of protein such as meat or poultry, eggs or cheese. Look for one of these as the first or second ingredient on a label. Animal-based protein is more digestible; that is, the dog's body can make better use of it than of grain-based sources of protein. Of course, not all animal-based sources of protein

Food dishes made of stainless steel are easy to clean.

are high in quality. Some examples of low-quality animal protein are collagen and feathers, which are poorly digestible. A food's digestibility level is not included on the label, but you can gauge it yourself by observing your dog's condition. Is its coat shiny? Does it produce small, firm feces? If your answer to these questions is yes, you can be assured that the food you're giving contains high-quality ingredients that meet your dog's needs.

Palatability and Price

Does your dog like the taste of its food? Palatability is an important concern. Dogs are individuals, and they have individual tastes and nutritional needs. A good food that suits one dog may not suit another.

Canned vs. dry. The question of canned vs. dry must also be considered. Each type has advantages and disadvantages. Naturally, most dogs find canned food more palatable than dry food, but canned food, once opened, spoils more quickly, is messy, and has an odor that isn't very appealing to people, although dogs seem to like it just fine. Dry food is less expensive and has a longer shelf life. Both canned and dry foods can provide high-quality nutrition, so make the choice after weighing your own preferences as well as the dog's. Of course, for the best of both worlds, you can always feed both.

Price. Another aspect of choosing a food is price. Unless you're independently wealthy, price will matter, but it shouldn't be the determining factor. You will save more money in the long run by feeding a high-quality food than by buying whatever's on sale or rock-bottom-price generic brands. Choose one brand that meets your dog's needs and is priced for your budget, and stick to it. To determine how much it costs to feed a certain brand each day, write the price on your calendar the day you start feeding it and track how long it lasts. Divide the cost by the number of days to get the cost per day. For instance, if a bag of food costs $19.99 and lasts for 15 days, its cost per day is $1.33.

Finally, take into account the manufacturer's responsiveness to consumers. Check the label for a toll-free number you can call if you have questions about ingredients, digestibility, or any other facet of dog nutrition.

Should You Give Supplements?

With the current emphasis on good health, it's natural to be concerned about whether a beloved pet is getting the proper amount of vitamins and minerals in its diet. That's understandable, since so many of us are guilty of eating more junk food and fewer fruits and vegetables than we should. Our dogs, however, are lucky enough to have available foods that are specially formulated to provide them with all their nutritional needs. That being the case, most veterinary nutritionists recommend against adding supplements to a dog's diet. Too much of a good thing is just as bad as a deficiency, and oversupplementation of vitamins and minerals—especially in puppyhood—can lead to skeletal disorders such as hip dysplasia, osteochondritis dissecans, and hypertrophic osteodystrophy (see Your Bloodhound's Health, beginning on page 75). These conditions are most common in large and giant breeds such as Bloodhounds. Unless your veterinarian recommends a supplement for a specific condition, avoid adding one to your dog's diet.

Nutritional No-Nos

Like most members of the hound family, Bloodhounds will eat just about anything, but that doesn't mean they should. Avoid giving your Bloodhound table scraps, raw meat and raw eggs, poultry, fish and pork bones, and toxic

If this dish were raised off the ground, it would be more comfortable for the Bloodhounds and would reduce the amount of air the dogs take in while eating, which may help prevent bloat.

substances such as alcohol and chocolate. Yes, chocolate in large amounts is toxic to dogs. It contains a chemical called theobromine to which dogs are unusually sensitive. Unsweetened baking chocolate has the highest amount of theobromine, but a dog that eats a

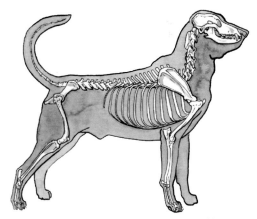

Bloodhound skeletal system. When your Bloodhound is at proper weight, you should be able to feel, but not see, its ribs beneath a layer of fat and muscle. An overweight Bloodhound is prone to serious orthopedic problems.

box of chocolate candy or gets into a Halloween stash is likely to receive a large dose. Signs of chocolate toxicosis usually occur four or five hours after the dog eats the chocolate and include vomiting, diarrhea, panting, restlessness, and muscle tremors. Given the Bloodhound's sensitive nose, you'll want to keep all chocolate out of reach.

As for the other no-nos, table scraps are usually high in fat and only encourage the dog to beg at the table, a habit that should not be permitted. Raw meat, poultry, and eggs may be infected with salmonella bacteria. Salmonella poisoning in dogs can cause vomiting and diarrhea, and is transmissible to people. The bones from fish, poultry, and pork can splinter easily and become lodged in the dog's throat. Like chocolate, alcohol can be toxic to dogs, and of course there is no reason to give it to them.

If you want to give your Bloodhound a treat, offer pieces of fresh fruits and vegetables. Many dogs love oranges, apples, bananas, grapes, carrots, and broccoli. These are healthy, low-calorie treats that you can give without a guilty conscience.

Keeping Your Bloodhound Trim

Obesity is one of the most common health problems affecting dogs. A survey of veterinarians shows that as many as a quarter of their canine patients are overweight. Obesity puts a dog at risk of such chronic health problems as diabetes, heart disease, and arthritis because of the extra stress placed on the joints.

A dog is defined as obese when it weighs 20 percent or more above its normal weight. You can tell if your Bloodhound is too fat by giving it the hands-on test. First, place both thumbs on the dog's backbone and spread your fingers along the rib cage. You should be able to feel the bony part of each rib beneath a slight layer of fat. As you stand over the dog, its waist should be visible behind the ribs and its abdomen tucked up behind the rib cage, giving it an hourglass figure. If your Bloodhound is shaped more like a can of dog food, it probably needs to go on a diet and get more exercise.

But before you make any changes in the dog's food or exercise level, take it to the veterinarian to make sure the excess weight doesn't have a medical cause, such as hypothyroidism. Once the dog has a clean bill of health, you and your veterinarian can develop a reducing plan that will help it lose weight safely. This may involve reducing the amount of food the dog receives or switching it to a low-calorie diet and gradually increasing the amount of physical activity.

Training

What Every Good Bloodhound Trainer Should Know

You've got to get up pretty early in the morning to stay ahead of a Bloodhound. Your Bloodhound is highly intelligent, but as a breed it has not been genetically selected for trainability. That means you need to think smart and think fast when dealing with your dog. Positive reinforcement with food rewards and praise are what will motivate your Bloodhound. Given the breed's dominant nature, it's unlikely to respond well at all to physical correction. Instead, be ready to provide a structured lifestyle that keeps the dog busy and focused. This includes frequent training sessions, regular exercise, and activities such as conformation shows, mantrailing trials and tracking tests, or search and rescue work.

There are secrets to successfully training a Bloodhound. As you train, keep these things in mind:

• *Be firm.* Firmness is not the same as meanness or physical roughness. Firmness means using a deep tone of voice that commands attention and respect. It does not mean repeating a command several times until your dog finally complies. Your dog must learn to pay attention the first time you speak, not to tune you out because you keep repeating the same thing over and over again. *Never hit or shake your Bloodhound,* and avoid trainers who advocate harsh methods.

• *Be consistent.* Don't use the same words for different actions or combine two conflicting commands. Your dog will only be confused when you tell it to *"Go sit down"* or say *"Get down"* when it jumps up on you. Use specific commands for each action, such as *"Sit," "Down,"* or *"Off."* Dogs are capable of learning many different words and phrases.

• *Develop a routine.* Your dog will learn best if commands are phrased in the same way each time. When you're training, say the dog's name and give the command immediately before the action takes place. That way, your dog learns to comply as soon as it hears the proper sequence of words. In mantrailing training, for instance, the *"Find"* command is given only when the Bloodhound is standing over the scent article, never at any other time.

• *Train when your dog is alert.* Most of us just want to take a nap after we eat, and our dogs are the same way. Schedule training sessions before meals. Consider the weather as well. Training in the heat of the day generally isn't a good idea unless you are acclimating a mantrailer that will need to work in all conditions.

• *Understand the psychology behind positive reinforcement.* Food treats and praise are tools that work only when used correctly. Hand them out lavishly when your dog is first learning, but increase your expectations and decrease the handouts as it becomes more proficient. So that it will always work at its best, your dog should never know when to expect a treat or praise. As an illustration, consider the difference between a vending machine and a slot machine. When we put 50 cents in a vending machine, we receive a package of corn chips and walk away. When we put 50 cents in a slot machine, sometimes we are rewarded with a payout and sometimes we're not. But the hope of hearing more quarters tumble out of the machine entices us into feeding more quarters into it. The hope of receiving a treat or praise will entice your dog into working harder for you.

• *Keep training sessions brief and upbeat.* Fifteen minutes is a good length. End the session at a point when your dog has been successful at the command or activity being practiced.

• *Never correct your dog after the fact.* Dogs do not share with us our sense of time. They don't connect a scolding with something they did five hours ago, or even five minutes ago. Unless you catch your dog in the act of misbehaving, save the angry words. If you do find your dog chewing, digging, or eliminating where it shouldn't, keep corrections short. Say "*No*" and either distract the dog with a toy or take it to the appropriate place to do its business. Then clean up the mess and get on with life with a Bloodhound.

When to Begin Training

Your puppy is capable of learning many new things at a rapid pace. The earlier you start training and socializing your Bloodhound, the better off you'll

Correct placement of the choke collar.

be. The ideal time to begin is when you bring it home at nine to twelve weeks of age. (Puppy training techniques and puppy kindergarten classes are discussed in greater detail on pages 30–32.) Once your pup has learned the basics, you can reinforce them with practical use at home, or you can go on to more advanced training for obedience trials or scent work.

Training Equipment

For puppy kindergarten, your Bloodhound will need nothing more than its flat leather or nylon collar and a leather or nylon leash that is ¾ inch (19 mm) wide and 5 to 6 feet (1.7–1.8 m) long. Be sure the collar is sized correctly. You should be able to fit two fingers between the collar and the dog's neck. Check the collar as your puppy grows to see if it needs to be adjusted.

Leash. Once it becomes used to it, the leash often becomes a dog's favorite item because it indicates a walk or other good times. The leash should be lightweight but well made, with a loop at one end for you to hold. Avoid chain leashes, which can be heavy and noisy.

Collar. When you move from puppy kindergarten into a regular obedience class, your trainer may or may not require the use of a training, or choke, collar. If used properly, a choke collar is an effective and harmless training tool, but many trainers today prefer to use as little negative reinforcement as possible. Run, don't walk, from any trainer who advocates choking or hanging the dog with this type of collar.

A training collar may be made of metal or nylon. For a dog the size of a Bloodhound, it should have medium-size links. Be sure you know how to put it on, or it won't release correctly. Place the collar so that the ring where the lead is attached is on the left side of the neck. To give a correction, simply snap and release the collar, using a quick motion. The intent is to get your dog's attention, not to choke it.

Immediately after every training session, remove the choke collar and replace it with the dog's regular collar. It's very easy for a training collar to get caught on a gate, crate, or even a bit of shrubbery and strangle the dog.

Harness. A harness encourages a dog to pull, so you won't want to get one unless you are training your Bloodhound for mantrailing or tracking exercises. Be sure the harness is of sturdy construction and fits the dog properly so it won't have any friction sores. In addition to the harness, you will need a 30- to 40-foot (9–12 m) tracking lead made of cotton webbing.

The Polite Bloodhound

By the time it is four to six months old, your Bloodhound should know the *sit, down, stay, sit/stay, down/stay,* and *come* commands. Instructions for teaching these commands are on pages 30 and 31. You can build on this foundation by extending the length of time required for the *stays,* and teaching new commands such as *"Wait"* (to slow down a dog that is pulling your arm out of its socket), *"Up"* (for getting into the car or onto a grooming table), and the directions for left and right.

As well as knowing these commands, your Bloodhound should be housetrained and have some understanding of what's okay to chew and what's not. That doesn't necessarily mean the Bloodhound won't chew up the patio furniture, just that it is somewhat less likely to if you have kept it occupied and provided it with interesting chew toys.

If all this isn't enough for you, consider providing your Bloodhound with higher education in the form of training for obedience trials, tracking tests, or mantrailing trials. The continuing structure and activity will be good for your dog, especially as it enters adolescence and early adulthood.

Obedience Trials

Bloodhounds are not known for their prowess in obedience trials, but with patient and persistent training they can succeed. In 1996, six Bloodhounds earned Companion Dog titles and two earned Utility Dog titles.

With patience, consistency, and praise, you can teach your Bloodhound to be a polite, lovable member of the family. Buckshot is 10 months old.

Obedience trials test a dog's ability to perform a specific set of exercises. Obedience titles can be earned at three levels: Novice, for the title Companion Dog; Open, for the title Companion Dog Excellent; and Utility, for the titles Utility Dog and Utility Dog Excellent. For each of these obedience titles, a dog must earn three "legs," meaning that it scores at least 170 out of a possible 200 points, with more than 50 percent on each exercise. A dog that earns a utility title can then accumulate points toward an obedience trial championship, but no Bloodhound has yet reached this pinnacle.

Dogs at the Novice level must heel on leash, stand for examination, heel free (off leash), come when called (recall), and perform a long sit (one minute) and a long down (three minutes). Open classes consist of the exercises heel free, drop on recall, retrieve on flat, retrieve over the high jump, broad jump, long sit (three minutes), and long down (five minutes). At the Utility level, the dog must complete a signal exercise (in which it is directed by hand signals with no verbal commands), two scent discrimination tests, a directed retrieve, a directed jump, and stand for group examination. Success in obedience trials is dependent on precise performance and timing.

Good Bloodhound Citizenship

If the precision required by obedience trials doesn't appeal to you and your Bloodhound, you may want to go for a Canine Good Citizen award instead. The Canine Good Citizen test rates dogs on their appearance and grooming; willingness to accept the approach of a stranger; ability to sit politely for petting, calm down after play or praise, walk on a loose leash, and walk through a crowd; performance of the *sit, down, stay,* and *come* commands; reactions to other dogs and distractions, and behavior when left alone. This is a less regimented series of exercises than those in obedience trials, and it is a good test of the skills and behavior every dog should exhibit.

If you need a little help in getting to that point, a trainer can help you prepare for the CGC test, which is usually offered several times a year by local dog clubs. When your Bloodhound earns this title, you can proudly put the initials CGC behind its name, secure in the knowledge that you have a well-behaved dog.

Common Behavior Problems

Aggression

Bloodhounds are not mean dogs, but for more than 1,000 years they have been selected for the ability to perform without human direction. This means they are independent and confident, expecting to do things their own way. These qualities do not translate to being a good pet, and a Bloodhound without an owner who provides strong leadership will soon make a play for the leadership role itself: pushing ahead of people, shoving them out of the way, guarding food and toys, and refusing to get off furniture. Other signs of aggression include ignoring commands and mounting you or other family members. These behaviors, especially jumping up, are often misinterpreted or ignored until one day the cute puppy has turned into a big dog that growls when its dominant behaviors are finally rebuffed. At this point, the help of a qualified behaviorist is usually necessary to straighten out the situation.

To prevent dominance aggression from ever getting to this stage, be alert for problem behaviors—especially if your dog displays three or more of them—when a puppy is young and still malleable. For instance, if the puppy pushes ahead of you through door-ways, teach it to sit at doorways until you give the signal to come. Instead of retreating when the puppy shoves you or humps your leg, push back, invad-ing its space. Forestall food guarding by frequently taking up a young pup-py's food and then returning it. Require the dog to sit before you feed it. Your actions teach the dog that you have the power over food, which is a pack leader prerogative.

Avoid physical force. Use a distrac-tion such as a toy or treat to lure the dog when it is misbehaving—for instance, refusing to get off the sofa—and then reward it when it comes to you. Then make sure it doesn't have the opportunity to get back on the sofa. The trick to successfully dealing with a Bloodhound is limiting its options.

Barking

This is not a common problem in Bloodhounds, but it can occur if they get bored or lonely. Try to determine why the dog is barking. Rotate toys to prevent boredom, and spend plenty of time with the dog. To deter barking, there are several methods you can try. If you are near the dog, wrap your hand around its muzzle and say "No bark" or "Quiet." Praise the dog for being quiet. A shake can works well when you are some distance from the dog. Take an empty soda can, put a few pennies in it, and tape the top closed. When the dog barks, throw the can in its direction (don't try to hit the dog). Ideally, the can will appear to come from nowhere. The noise will startle the dog so it stops barking. Then praise it for being quiet.

For times when you can't be there, a bark-inhibiting collar may work. These collars usually work by giving off a high-frequency sound when the dog barks. Like a shake can, the sound is intended to distract the dog so that it stops barking. A new collar has been

developed that emits a mist of citronella every time the dog barks. The scent discourages the dog from barking.

Chewing

Bloodhounds love to chew, and they'll chew on anything. Attempt to control this habit from the beginning by directing your dog toward appropri-ate chew toys while it's young. Keep valued items away from those inquir-ing jaws, and rotate toys frequently so your dog doesn't get bored. If you see your dog chewing on something it shouldn't, take the item away (without making a fuss) and replace it with an acceptable toy. Then praise the dog for chewing on the toy. Some chewers are deterred by the application of Bit-ter Apple or hot sauce to plants, furni-ture, and other items, while others just find that it adds to the flavor.

Digging

This is another favorite Bloodhound activity, usually initiated by boredom or the scenting of buried treasure. Dig-ging is fun for dogs, and it's an ingrained canine habit. Rather than try-ing to stop it altogether, your best bets may be to channel your dog's energies in other ways or to direct digging to places that are acceptable to you.

Frequent, regular playtime, walks, and training sessions will help keep your dog so busy it doesn't have the time or energy to dig. If this isn't possi-ble, stake out a play area where it's okay for the dog to dig, such as a sandbox. Stud the area with toys to make it enticing. If you see your dog digging where it shouldn't, simply take it to the play area. When it digs there, give lots of praise and encouragement.

Inappropriate Elimination

If your dog is six months or older, has plenty of opportunities to go out-side and eliminate, yet still has acci-dents in the house, your first step

Scent-marking is a dog's way of claiming territory. While it's not bothersome outdoors, it is obnoxious in the house and is best controlled by neutering before the dog is a year old.

A Bloodhound can knock people over when it jumps up on them. Teach your Bloodhound to sit for petting instead, or to jump up only when invited.

should be to take it to the veterinarian to make sure there is nothing physically wrong with it. For instance, spayed females sometimes "leak," a condition that can be controlled with medication. Older dogs may not have the bladder control of their younger years, which isn't something they should be punished for. Put down papers for them to use, or limit them to areas that are easily cleaned.

If the dog is healthy, repeat the housetraining process by keeping the dog on a strict feeding and elimination schedule. When you can't be there to supervise, put the dog in its crate or in a confined area with newspapers laid down. Observe the dog carefully for signs that it needs to go out. Some dogs are very subtle in expressing their needs, giving only a brief whine or even just an expectant look when they need to eliminate.

Excitement or excessive submission can also cause dogs to lose control of their bladders. To help put a stop to this behavior, keep homecomings low-key, and greet the dog down at its level instead of standing over it. Often, submissive urination is outgrown.

The territorial marking of urine, especially by males, is best controlled by neutering at an early age. Otherwise, use a shake can or water squirter to startle the dog when it starts to lift its leg, and buy lots of stock in companies that make odor-control products.

Jumping Up

Most people incorrectly view jumping up by a dog as an expression of welcome, but it's a dominant behavior that should be discouraged, especially in such a large breed. Teach your puppy that jumping up will be ignored, but sitting is rewarded. If your dog jumps up on you, step back or turn aside so it doesn't make contact. Then tell the dog to sit. When it complies, give plenty of praise.

Understanding Dog Shows

What Is a Dog Show?

The AKC sponsors a number of different types of competitive events. The most popular of these are conformation shows, in which dogs are judged on how closely they measure up to the standard for their breed.

Many people think of the dog show simply as a beauty contest, but there's more to it than that. The intent of a conformation show is for breeders to display the dogs resulting from their breeding programs so they can be judged on their physical and mental soundness, as well as how they stack up against the standard. The best of these earn the title of champion and are the dogs to whom other breeders want to mate their dogs.

All-Breed and Specialty Shows

There are two types of conformation shows: all-breed and specialty. More than 1,200 all-breed shows took place in 1996, with 1,374,378 dogs competing; there were almost 2,000 specialty shows, with 148,386 dogs competing. Any of the breeds recognized by the AKC may enter all-breed shows, which are held by local all-breed clubs. Specialty shows are limited to one specific breed, such as Bloodhounds, and are held by local specialty clubs or the breed's national parent club. In 1997, the American Bloodhound Club held its largest specialty ever, with 209 entries from all over the United States and Canada. The five-day show included conformation classes, obedience trials, a puppy sweepstakes competition,

an AKC tracking trial, and an ABC mantrailing trial. A national specialty is a great opportunity for Bloodhound fanciers to socialize with one another, swap stories about their dogs' exploits on and off the trail, and see the breed's best dogs in competition. At the 1997 national specialty, 63 champion Bloodhounds competed in the Best of Breed ring, with a Bloodhound from Canada ultimately taking the title of Best in Specialty show.

Watching a Dog Show

The first time you attend a dog show, it may seem confusing, but think of it as a process of elimination. Dogs compete against each other in various classes. Then the class winners compete against each other until

This is a black-and-tan Bloodhound with the noble, dignified appearance that is characteristic of the breed.

one is chosen Best of Breed. At an all-breed show, the breed winners then compete in their respective groups (Sporting, Hound, Working, Terrier, Toy, Non-Sporting, and Herding), with one winner being chosen from each group. There are also second-, third-, and fourth-place winners in Group competition. Finally, all the Group winners meet in the ring to determine which dog will be named Best in Show.

You may be wondering how it's possible to judge one breed against another. It seems as if it would be comparing apples and oranges. That's where the standard comes in. The breeds are judged not against each other but against their respective standards. The judge's job is to choose the dog that most closely meets its standard. (See below.)

Following a Bloodhound through the Show

There are five classes in which non-champion Bloodhounds may be entered at shows: Puppy, Novice, Bred-by-Exhibitor, American-Bred, and Open. Sometimes puppy classes are subdivided into Puppies six to nine months and Puppies nine to twelve months. In all classes, males compete against males and females against females. Once each class has a winner, they all compete in the Winners class, again separated by sex. A Winners Dog and Winners Bitch are chosen, as well as a Reserve Winners Dog and Reserve Winners Bitch. The Reserve Winners will take the points if for some reason the win of the Winners Dog or Bitch is disallowed.

Next, Bloodhounds that are already champions, plus the Winners Dog and Winners Bitch, compete in the Best of Breed class. The judge also decides Best of Winners between the Winners Dog and Winners Bitch. If the Winners Dog or Bitch was named

Best of Breed, it automatically becomes Best of Winners. Finally, the judge selects Best of Opposite Sex, which is just what it sounds like: the best dog of the sex opposite that of the Best of Breed winner. Then, as described above, the Best of Breed winner goes through Group competition and, if it's lucky, Best-in-Show judging. At some shows, as many as 4,000 dogs may compete in a single day for this coveted award.

Points

To earn a championship, a dog must accumulate 15 points at shows. The number of points earned at each show depends on how many dogs were entered for that breed. Because some breeds are more numerous and found in a greater number of areas than others, the number of dogs required for points is based on the breed, sex, and show location. Depending on these variables, a dog may earn from one to five points per show. A win that carries three, four, or five points is called a *major*. The points accumulated toward a championship must include wins from three different judges and at least two majors from different judges. In 1996, 83 Bloodhounds earned championships.

The Bloodhound Standard

A breed standard is a written description of the physical characteristics of the ideal dog. It is what separates a Bloodhound from a Basset Hound from a Beagle. Each breed has a standard, against which it is judged in the show ring. No dog will meet the standard in all respects; the winner is the dog that most closely meets the standard. Careful breeders know the standard by heart and use it to help make decisions about which Bloodhounds to breed to each other to improve the appearance and soundness of the dogs they produce.

A breed standard is not immutable. It may change over the years to permit new colors or to clarify a point that is confusing. Any changes made to the standard are initiated by a breed's parent club and must be voted on and approved by the membership. Then the changes are sent to the AKC's board of directors for their approval. A copy of the current Bloodhound standard is available by writing to the American Kennel Club (address on page 92) and requesting the *Official Standard of the Bloodhound* pamphlet. Some of the terms used in the standard are explained in the boxed glossary on page 54.

Scenting Ability and General Appearance

The Bloodhound standard begins by describing the breed's general character and appearance. Not surprisingly, the very first sentence mentions the breed's powerful scenting ability: "The Bloodhound possesses, in a most marked degree, every point and characteristic of those dogs which hunt together by scent (Sagaces)." It goes on to say that the Bloodhound is very powerful and stands over more ground than is usual with hounds of other breeds. The phrase "standing over more ground" means that the Bloodhound is slightly longer in body than other scenthounds. Next, the standard says that the skin is thin to the touch and extremely loose, especially around the head and neck, where it hangs in deep folds. In these few words, we have a pretty good general description of the Bloodhound: a large dog with folds of loose skin about the head and neck, known for its ability to hunt by scent. The rest of the standard spells out details such as height, weight, and color, and points out differences between males (dogs) and females (bitches).

Height. The mean average height of adult dogs is 26 inches (66 cm), while that of adult bitches is 24 inches (61 cm). Dogs usually vary from 25 inches (63.5 cm) to 27 inches (68.5 cm), and bitches from 23 inches (58 cm) to 25 inches (63.5 cm). In either case, the standard says, the greater height is to be preferred, as long as the dog also has character and quality.

Weight. The mean average weight of adult dogs in fair condition is 90 pounds (41 kg), with adult bitches being 80 pounds (36 kg). Dogs may weigh as much as 110 pounds (50 kg), bitches 100 pounds (45 kg). Just as with height, the greater weights are preferred, if quality and proportion are there as well. In the case of both weight and height, the phrase "the greater height/weight is to be preferred" should not be interpreted to mean that the Bloodhound should be taller or heavier than the maximum measurements given here.

Expression and temperament. Even expression and temperament are covered by the standard. A Bloodhound's expression should be noble and dignified, characterized by solemnity, wisdom, and power. In temperament, a Bloodhound is extremely affectionate, neither quarrelsome with companions nor with other dogs. Its nature is somewhat shy, and it is equally sensitive to kindness or correction by its master. Never should a Bloodhound be aggressive or fearful.

Other physical characteristics described by the standard include the shape and properties of the head and face, position of the eyes and ears, and proper style of body, legs, feet, and tail.

Head. The head of a Bloodhound is narrow in proportion to its length and long in proportion to the body, tapering slightly from the temples to the end of the muzzle. When viewed from above and in front, the head has the

The Bloodhound's loose skin helps protect the dog from injury as it moves through heavy brush.

In profile, the upper outline of the skull should be nearly in the same plane as that of the foreface. This Bloodhound's head planes are not correct.

appearance of being flattened at the sides and of being nearly equal in width throughout its entire length. In profile, the upper outline of the skull is nearly in the same plane as that of the foreface. The length from end of nose to stop (midway between the eyes) should be not less than that from stop to back of occipital protuberance (peak). The entire length of head from the back part of the occipital protuberance to the end of the muzzle should be 12 inches (30 cm) or more in dogs, 11 inches (28 cm) or more in bitches.

Skull and face. The skull is long and narrow, with a pronounced occipital peak. The brows are not prominent, although they may appear so because of the deep-set eyes. The Bloodhound has a long, deep foreface, of even width throughout, with a square outline when seen in profile. A Bloodhound puppy at a show once demonstrated this square outline—indicating proper depth of lip—when he snagged a can of beer on the way into the ring. Because his lips were so deep, the can went unnoticed until the judge's examination. Depth of lip is important because it is the lip that keeps the nasal area moist so the olfactory membrane functions well.

Eyes. Its eyes are one of the Bloodhound's most well-known characteristics. They are deeply sunk in the orbits, and the lids have a lozenge or diamond shape. This is because the lower lids are dragged down and turned outward by the heavy flews. This can cause eye problems if the flews are too heavy, so a good breeder goes for moderation rather than exaggeration. The eye color ranges from deep hazel to yellow, corresponding with the general tone of the dog's color. The deep hazel color is preferred.

Ears. Another distinctive characteristic of the Bloodhound is its ears. They are thin and soft to the touch, extremely·long, and set very low—

below the level of the eye—falling in graceful folds with the lower parts curling inward and backward. The long ears, too, are functional, sweeping the scent up toward the nose.

Skin. Someone who didn't know the Bloodhound might assume that the dog shrank in the wash, causing its skin not to fit, but the standard tells us that the heavy wrinkles and apparently excess skin are correct. The head, it says, is furnished with an amount of loose skin, which in nearly every position appears superabundant, but more particularly so when the head is carried low; the skin then falls into loose, pendulous ridges and folds, especially over the forehead and sides of the face. All this loose skin serves a serious purpose: It protects the dog from scrapes and scratches when it is moving through briars or heavy foliage, and it helps the Bloodhound retain the scent for further reference.

Bite. In front, the lips fall squarely, making a right angle with the upper line of the foreface, while behind they form deep, hanging flews, and being continued into the pendant folds of loose skin about the neck, constitute the dewlap, which is very pronounced. These characteristics are found, though in a lesser degree, in the bitch. For the mouth, a scissors bite is preferred, but a level bite is accepted.

Nostrils. Last but not least on the head are the nostrils, which are described as large and open. The wideness of the nostrils helps the Bloodhound pick up scent.

Body. Moving on to the body, the standard describes the neck, shoulders, chest, back, and loin. The neck should be long. This is important, because it allows the dog to drop its head down to follow a scent while still moving well. The shoulders are muscular and well sloped backward, the ribs are well sprung, and the chest is well let down between the forelegs,

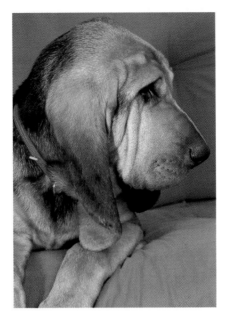

The Bloodhound's long head and wide foreface provide plenty of room for turbinates, the specialized cells in the nasal cavity that feed information about various odors to the brain via the olfactory nerve.

forming a deep keel. The back and loins are strong, with the loins being deep and slightly arched.

Legs and feet. Of course, for a dog that spends as much time on the move as the Bloodhound, legs and feet are of prime importance. The

A proper Bloodhound moves purposefully, with a gait that is elastic, swinging, and free, but not sloppy.

53

Standard Definitions

Hock: In simple terms, the dog's heel. It is a collection of bones of the hind leg, which form the joint between the second thigh (the area on the hind leg between the knee and the hock) and the metatarsus.

Hocks well let down: Hock joints are short, or close to the ground.

Keel: The rounded outline of the lower chest.

Loin: Located behind the ribs and in front of the pelvic girdle.

Occipital protuberance: A high, or raised, occiput. This characteristic is found in several hound and sporting breeds.

Occiput: The back part of the skull.

Pastern: The area of the foreleg between the wrist and toes.

Splayed feet: Feet that are flat with the toes spread out.

Stop: The indentation between the eyes where the nasal bones and cranium meet.

Well-sprung ribs: Indicates curvature of the ribs. Well-sprung ribs allow for plenty of heart and lung capacity, which are important for endurance on the trail.

forelegs should be straight and large in bone, with elbows squarely set. The thighs and second thighs (gaskins) are very muscular, with the hocks being well bent and let down and squarely set. The feet should be strong and well knuckled up. Naturally, the pads of the feet should be thick to protect the dog from injury on the trail. Some faults of the legs and feet are weak pasterns and splayed feet.

Gait. The Bloodhound's gait—the way it moves—should be elastic, swinging, and free. This does not mean, however, that the dog's gait should be loose or sloppy. Rather than flailing around, the legs should be moving with a purpose. Nor should the hocks turn in as the dog moves, with the rear feet toeing out. A dog that moves this way is described as cow-hocked. At a moderate trot, the Bloodhound's forelegs should move in a straight line from shoulder to foot, the rear legs in a straight line from hip to foot. The feet should come together toward a center line without crossing.

Tail. Even the appearance of the tail is important in the standard. The tail, also called the stern, should be long and tapering, set on rather high, with a moderate amount of hair underneath. As the Bloodhound moves, its tail is carried high, but shouldn't be curled too much over the back.

Color. In color, the Bloodhound may be black and tan, liver and tan, or red. The darker colors are sometimes interspersed with lighter or badger-colored hair, and sometimes flecked with white. A small amount of white is permissible on the chest, feet, and tip of stern.

The overall appearance of a Bloodhound should be one of refinement, not coarseness. The dog's features, while striking, should not be exaggerated, nor should the dog be overly large or heavy.

Showing Your Bloodhound

Competing with a Bloodhound in the conformation ring requires a sense of humor and a lot of patience, but it can be very rewarding. A nice Bloodhound that is presented properly is not difficult to finish to a championship. The following tips will help you successfully meet the challenge of showing this breed.

1. Ask your breeder or another person knowledgeable about Bloodhounds to evaluate your dog. Of course it looks beautiful to you, but a more clear-eyed evaluation can help you decide if being shown is really

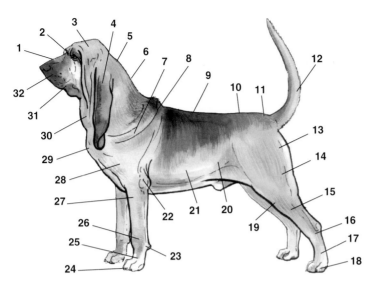

External anatomy of the Bloodhound.

1. nose bridge
2. stop
3. skull
4. ear
5. crest
6. neck
7. shoulder
8. withers
9. back
10. loin
11. rump (croup)
12. tail
13. hindquarters
14. upper thigh
15. lower thigh
16. hock
17. pastern
18. hind foot
19. stifle
20. flank
21. brisket
22. elbow
23. dewclaw
24. paw
25. fore foot
26. wrist
27. forearm
28. upper arm
29. point of shoulder
30. throat
31. flews
32. muzzle

right for your dog. In addition to correct structure and physical soundness, a show-quality Bloodhound has that special something known as star quality. It is curious, assertive, and brave, always out there investigating, with its tail up.

2. Attend handling classes to learn ring etiquette and how to present your dog. Working to establish leash control and a rapport with the dog are the most important things you can do. It's unreasonable to expect perfect control over your Bloodhound in the ring, but you can learn to work with it instead of against it. That way, the two of you will look less like Laurel and Hardy and more like Ginger and Fred.

3. Never get angry with your Bloodhound when things don't go as planned. Instead, try to figure out how you can make its quirks work for you. Setting the lead the same way each time you go in the ring, keeping a special toy handy to hold your dog's attention, and adjusting your stride

and direction to that of the dog will help you maintain a smooth and professional appearance. Praise your dog for the things it does well, and accept the things it won't do well.

4. Present a clean, attractive, comfortable dog. Bathe your dog before the show to temporarily reduce that houndy odor. Pay special attention to the feet, ears, and all the loose skin around the head, which are the areas most likely to produce odor. Carry a slobber towel in the ring so your dog's mouth is dry for the judge's examination. Be sure your dog is kept cool before it goes in the ring so it's not already panting and uncomfortable when it walks in.

5. Look professional. The Bloodhound has a reputation as a slobbery clown, but you can add a touch of class by dressing appropriately and presenting a well-groomed dog. Leave your jeans and T-shirt at home.

6. Avoid using bait. Liver and other treats simply cause your dog to drool

Any time your Bloodhound has been in a wooded or grassy area, search it carefully for ticks.

more. And in the case of a dog that is fixated on food, bait can cause it to misbehave or to become aggressive toward the other dogs in an attempt to guard its treat.

7. Prevent boredom. While other dogs are being judged, let yours play with a toy or visit with fans at ringside. Let it know what a good time the two of you are having. When it's your turn with the judge, the dog will have gotten the silliness out of its system and can focus on the job at hand.

8. Make showing fun. Your Bloodhound should want to be in the ring more than anything else because you've made it feel special and important. The best show dogs are attuned to applause, and they go around the ring with tail up, playing to the crowd, enjoying what they're doing. The Bloodhound is the comedian of the Hound Group, and you can use that to your advantage.

9. Present your dog, not yourself. The best handlers are the ones you don't even notice. They know that their job is to make the dog look good and to make the judge think as much of the dog as they do. Remember that the judge is looking at the dog, not at you.

10. Keep in mind that your dog is always a winner, no matter how you place, so never show disappointment as you walk out of the ring. Your dog will pick up on your manner. Instead, tell it what a good dog it is and give it a toy. Showing will go better if you and the dog always have a good time.

The Bloodhound at Work

Mantrailing

In movie after movie, packs of Bloodhounds are seen running down escaped criminals, their bell-like voices baying their excitement. What the audience doesn't see after the director yells "Cut!" is the Bloodhound finally reaching its quarry and planting slobbery kisses on its face. In the words of one law enforcement officer to the escaped convicts on whom he was holding his gun: "You better let my dog kiss you; it's his reward."

The thrill of the hunt and the joy of success are the only things motivating a Bloodhound on the trail. To this dog, trailing is a game, and it works for the sheer pleasure of winning the game: making a find, whether it be a lost child, an elderly person who has wandered away from a nursing home, or a dangerous felon. Although it has a fearsome reputation, the Bloodhound is truly a sweetheart, wanting only to make friends with this new person it has found.

Because of their film image, Bloodhounds are perhaps best known for tracking down escaped convicts, but they are also deployed when people are lost or crimes have been committed. Nationwide, 3,000 to 5,000 Bloodhounds have found a place with volunteer search and rescue teams, municipal law enforcement officers, county sheriff departments, state agencies, and state and federal prison systems.

Training a Mantrailer

The search for a puppy suitable for mantrailing begins in early puppyhood.

Trainers examine litters carefully, looking for that special pup that's curious and nosy, spending more time investigating its environment than playing with littermates. This pup is strongly attracted to people, noticing immediately when they're around, and isn't afraid of loud noises or sudden movements. In addition to having the right personality, a puppy must also be physically sound, with a good likelihood that it will measure up to the standard when it matures. From its large headpiece to the thick pads on its feet, the Bloodhound is a functional dog, designed to follow a scent trail. If its neck is too short or its paw pads too thin, the dog won't be able to do a good job. A Bloodhound that is successful

The Bloodhound's sensitive nose picks up clues from ground and air when it's on the trail of a missing person or a fugitive. Even trails that have grown "cold" don't baffle this consummate sleuth.

I am the dog world's best detective.
My sleuthing nose is so effective
I sniff the guilty at a distance,
And then they lead a doomed
  existence.
  —Edward Anthony, *The Bloodhound*

on the trail should be just as successful in the show ring.

Training begins as early as ten weeks of age and continues throughout the dog's life. There is always something new to learn. A Bloodhound must run four trails a week for at least a year before it's considered to be capable of going out and handling a real-life incident.

Teaching a pup to follow a scent trail requires plenty of positive reinforcement. Food treats are used to entice the young pup. First, the person laying the trail gives the puppy a sniff of the treat, then backs away, all the while calling the pup by name. When the trail layer is about 10 feet (3 m) away, he or she drops a scent article and continues walking away. Then the handler takes the puppy to the scent article and gives a starting command, such as "*Go find.*" The starting command can be any word or phrase, but it should be used only at the beginning of a trail, never at any other time. The dog must learn to associate the command with the scent it is standing over at that given time, ensuring that it always locks in on and follows the correct scent.

At first, the puppy works by sight, because the trail layer is only 100 to 150 feet (30–46 m) ahead. When the pup reaches the person, it is given the treat and heaped with praise. Then the exercise is repeated three times. After three or four days of this, the trail layer adds a 90-degree turn to the trail, which remains the same length. Now the pup must start relying on its nose, since the trail layer is no longer in sight.

Once the puppy is successful at this stage, the game gradually becomes

more difficult. For instance, the next step would be to start the pup over a scent article after the trail layer has already left. Then the age and length of the trail are extended. The trainer may add problems for the pup to solve, such as multiple trail layers with a scent article from only one of them, or starting from a known location rather than a definite scent article. A real-world application of this ability might be when a suspect is spotted walking by a certain landmark. The area is kept uncontaminated by the scent of other people until the dog arrives to start the trail. For a Bloodhound that will make its living as a professional, the hide-and-seek games it learns as a pup are involved and intense brainteasers.

Adequate training is important for the handler as well. At the other end of the leash must be a person who trusts the dog, communicates well with it, and can read the dog's actions. Lack of confidence in a dog's abilities has in many instances meant red faces when it is later discovered that the dog was right all along. The credibility of all Bloodhounds and their handlers is damaged when inexperienced teams attempt to work a trail at the professional level.

Conditioning a Mantrailer

Regular training sessions combined with the average day's routine of play and other activity is enough to keep most mantrailing Bloodhounds in good physical condition. In addition to regular exercise, though, they must be acclimated to all weather conditions. Dedicated handlers work their dogs regardless of the weather. A Bloodhound may be needed to work on a hot summer day or during a thunderstorm. That means that training must take place during these conditions as well, so that the dog is ready to go at any time, any season.

Working the Trail

Ideal scenting conditions are 40 to 60°F (4.4–15.5°C) with moisture in the air as well as on the ground. A light rain or the presence of dew on the ground increases the bacterial activity on the skin cells that make up scent. When the temperature drops below this range, bacterial activity decreases, meaning that less scent is available. Bacterial activity also decreases when temperatures are high and the climate is arid. This makes scenting more difficult in hot, dry areas.

A common misconception is that rain washes scent away. Rather, moisture refreshes a scent and makes it stronger. If a trail was laid during the heat of the day, it's sometimes more productive to wait until nightfall, when the temperature drops.

In the movie *Cool Hand Luke,* Paul Newman sprinkles curry powder, pepper, and other spices on the ground, sending the Bloodhounds that run across it into a fit of sneezing and throwing them off his trail. But that only works in the movies—vanilla, creosote, and spices do nothing to deter a Bloodhound. As long as the person being tracked is on foot, the Bloodhound will stay on the trail.

Another fallacy promoted by the entertainment industry is that going through water throws the dogs off the scent. The human body—dead or alive—gives off scent, even in water, where it hangs on the surface and collects on vegetation. Bloodhounds have been taken out in boats many times to locate drowning victims. When the hound leans to the left, the pilot steers left. When the hound leans to the right, the boat is steered to the right. When the hound wants to jump in the water, that's usually where the victim's body is found.

Finally, Bloodhounds bark only in the movies. True working Bloodhounds are silent on trail. If they barked, it would

announce their presence and location, a dangerous prospect in the case of desperate criminals. The knowledge could allow them to make good their escape by speeding up and getting a ride, or to double back around and try to ambush their followers.

Criminal Activity

When convicted assassin James Earl Ray escaped from Tennessee's Brushy Mountain State Prison in 1977, it was two Bloodhound bitches that found him. Besides tracking escaped convicts, Bloodhounds assist law enforcement officers in many other ways. They can indicate the direction a suspect took after committing a crime, whether a vehicle was involved, where it was parked, and in what direction it traveled, and find articles with fingerprint evidence that the suspect has dropped on the trail.

A Bloodhound can even reveal whether a series of crimes was committed by one or more people. For instance, if three burglaries take place overnight in the same town, the investigating officer can make a scent pad at the point of entry of each burglary. The dog is worked at each scene, following the burglar's trail to its end point. Then the scent articles are rotated, with scent article A taken to burglary site B, and the dog is started on the scent again. If the dog indicates that no trail leads away from the scene, the investigator knows that the burglaries were committed by two different people. If the dog runs the same trail it did the

A working Bloodhound spends a lot of time on the road, going to trailing sites or practice sessions.

When the harness goes on, the Bloodhound knows it's time to go to work.

This K-9 team is assembled and ready to roll.

Once on the trail, the Bloodhound is hard to hold back. It takes a long line and a handler in good shape to keep up.

first time, it indicates that burglaries A and B were committed by the same person. The process is repeated at the site of burglary C. The information by itself probably won't solve the crime—it's rare to have a walk-up find in the case of a burglary—but the additional knowledge gives the investigator an edge in solving the crime.

Sometimes Bloodhounds are used in lineup situations. Take the proverbial case of an armed robbery in which the perpetrator drops his ski mask. If a suspect is later arrested, he is placed in a lineup, and the dog is started off the scent from the ski mask. If the dog goes from the scent article to the suspect, the case goes to court. In such a situation, the Bloodhound is simply following a very short trail and using its powers of scent discrimination to select the person giving off a scent that matches that of the ski mask.

Testifying in Court

The power and accuracy of the Bloodhound's nose is so highly respected that many courts accept its testimony. The famous Bloodhound Nick Carter had more than 650 convictions to his credit. In most states, Bloodhound evidence is admissible in court as long as certain conditions are

When it has successfully completed a search and identified the "rabbit," a Bloodhound is rewarded with treats and praise.

Mantrailing is hot work. It's important to keep the Bloodhound hydrated.

Many Bloodhound owners find search and rescue work rewarding.

Jethro, a 10-month-old Bloodhound, is in training to become a search and rescue dog.

met, usually AKC registration and proof of adequate training. AKC registration verifies that the dog in question is indeed a Bloodhound. Proof of training is evidenced by the handler's training records or by work in previous cases.

Some states, however, consider use of Bloodhound evidence a gray area. Unlike the find made by a drug-sniffing dog, in which the drugs are used as evidence that a suspect possessed illegal substances, the find made by a Bloodhound can seem intangible; in essence, the prosecution is using the Bloodhound to say that a given person was at the scene of a crime, walked a certain route, and ended up at point B.

But even in states where Bloodhound evidence is not admissible in court, it has been used to obtain search warrants or to induce suspects to confess.

Sporting Events

If you simply want to enjoy your dog's abilities at the sport level, there are two events in which you can have fun outdoors and put titles on your dog: mantrailing trials and tracking tests. Mantrailing trials are held by the American Bloodhound Club and are limited to Bloodhounds, while tracking tests are AKC events that are open to any breed. Each event has three different levels to test a dog's abilities.

Mantrailing Trials

In this event, a Bloodhound can earn the titles Mantrailer (MT), Mantrailer Intermediate (MTI), and Mantrailer Excellent (MTX). For the MT title, the dog must successfully run a trail that is four hours old and a half-mile (.8 km) long. The MTI trail is 12 to 18 hours old, a mile (1.6 km) in length, with one cross runner. The MTX is the most difficult trail. It must be 24 to 36 hours old, a mile and a half (2.4 km) in length, with a cross runner who is within 15 feet (4.6 m) of the actual runner at the finish. To be successful, the dog must identify which person it followed to the end of the trail.

Tracking Tests

As with mantrailing trials, tracking tests require a dog to follow a trail by scent to earn Tracking Dog (TD), Tracking Dog Excellent (TDX), or Variable Surface Tracking (VST) titles. In the TD test, the track is 440 to 500 yards (402–457 m) long, with a minimum of two right-angle turns, and must be a half hour to two hours old. The person laying the track must be unknown to the dog. At the end of the track, the dog must locate a scent article dropped by the track layer. The TDX track is 800 to 1,000 yards (731–914 m) long, with several turns and two cross tracks. It must be three to five hours old and includes varying terrain such as ditches, streambeds, and tall grass. Dummy scent articles are laid along the trail. Tracking Dog and Tracking Dog Excellent tests usually take place in rural locations, but the VST tests a dog's tracking ability in more developed areas. The VST track length is 600 to 800 yards (548.6–731.5 m) and must cover a minimum of three types of surfaces, such as asphalt, concrete, grass, gravel, or sand. One-third to one-half of the track must be lacking in vegetation. The track must be three to five hours old with four to eight turns. A dog that passes all three tests earns the title Champion Tracker (CT).

It's important to remember that a dog successful in mantrailing trials and tracking tests should not be considered trained at the professional level. The skills required by a police Bloodhound are different than those required for success in sporting events. For more information about the rules and regulations for mantrailing trials and tracking tests, contact the ABC and the AKC (addresses on page 92).

Search and Rescue

To challenge your dog's abilities beyond the sport level, consider becoming involved in a search and rescue organization. Most search and rescue situations involve looking for lost hikers or wandering children. This can be an exciting and rewarding volunteer activity if your dog is properly trained and you have the orienteering and survival skills required. Members of search and rescue teams—and their dogs—must be in good shape and ready to go at any hour of the day or night.

Breeding Your Bloodhound

The Responsibilities of Breeding

Deciding to breed your Bloodhound is a serious undertaking. You will be responsible for bringing new lives into the world, and the dogs you produce will affect how other people perceive the Bloodhound breed. A serious breeder must ensure that the health of the bitch and dog is at its peak, that both dogs meet the standard and have qualities that are worthy of being reproduced, and that the puppies go to homes where they will be loved and cherished for a lifetime.

While breeding may seem like a fun hobby, a good way to get another puppy just like Daisy, or even a way to recoup the cost of purchasing Daisy, you will find that much more work, expense, and heartache are involved than you ever dreamed possible. Pregnancy and whelping can have long-term negative effects on your bitch's personality—as can the act of mating for a male—and can even cost her life. Before you go any further, think long and hard about your reasons for breeding and the risks you are willing to take.

When Should You Breed?

Your bitch should not be bred before she is two years old. She will then be fully mature physically and emotionally, and it is the earliest she can receive certifications for good hips, elbows, and eyes. Because conditions such as hip dysplasia, elbow dysplasia, and entropion and ectropion are hereditary in nature, no Bloodhound should be bred whose hips and elbows have not been X-rayed and certified as good or excellent by the Orthopedic Foundation for Animals (OFA). Eye condition must be passed by the Canine Eye Registration Foundation, or CERF.

Of course, your bitch should be current on her vaccinations, free of internal parasites, and tested for brucellosis, a sexually transmitted disease. (The stud should also be tested for brucellosis.) Ideally, your veterinarian will be knowledgeable about breeding so he or she can advise you about potential whelping problems such as a narrow pelvis. Naturally, your Bloodhound's conformation should meet the standard, with no flaws such as mismarkings, a kinked tail, paper-thin feet, or an undershot jaw. Your breeder can help you determine whether Daisy—or Rufus—is a suitable candidate for breeding.

Ensuring that a bitch is healthy and ready for breeding can cost as much as $1,000. And don't forget the other half of the equation. Stud dogs should meet the same high standards of age, conformation, and health. A responsible stud owner will be just as concerned as you are that your bitch's qualities are a good match with those of his or her male. Expect to be asked why you want to breed your bitch, whether you already have deposits for the puppies that will be produced, how you plan to raise the pups, and whether you have tested for genetic defects.

When you are choosing a bitch or stud, remember that titles and heavy advertising are not everything. Some fine dogs never finish their championships, while many mediocre dogs do. Look at the whole dog, and study its pedigree carefully before making a decision.

A Breeding Plan

Before you breed, write out your goals as a breeder. What good characteristics do you want to fix in your line, and what bad characteristics do you want to eliminate? A good breeding plan should look at least three generations ahead. Think about what kind of puppies you can expect from the breeding you have planned and where you will go with those puppies.

It's also important to learn about types of breeding. Linebreeding, inbreeding, and outcrossing are terms you should know and understand.

Linebreeding. Linebreeding is a way to fix good characteristics and to express bad characteristics that need to be eliminated. It is defined as breeding related dogs within a line or family to a common ancestor. For example, you might breed a male to his grandmother or a bitch to her grandfather. Linebreeding works well when you are breeding two high-quality dogs with the goal of enhancing a particular attribute such as a good head or strong feet. That said, it's important to remember that you should always focus on the whole dog in your breeding plan. In your quest for the perfect head, don't lose sight of the rest of the body.

Inbreeding. Inbreeding is the mating of dogs that are even more closely related than in linebreeding, such as mother to son or sister to brother. People who are uninformed about genetics and breeding techniques often blame problems in dogs on inbreeding or predict puppies with two heads and six legs. Inbreeding in and of itself does not create defects, but it does allow defects to be expressed. Done knowledgeably, however, inbreeding is a valid approach that can produce healthy, high-quality puppies. The secret to successful inbreeding is the use of two dogs with excellent attributes and few or minor flaws. The attributes will be intensified, but conversely; so will flaws be magnified. Breeders who choose inbreeding must be conversant with the entire pedigrees of both dogs involved, aware of all the health and conformation problems that could pop up, and prepared to deal with those ramifications.

Outcrossing. Breeding two unrelated dogs is called outcrossing. An outcross may be called for if you wish to introduce a desirable characteristic into your line. Crossing two unrelated line-bred dogs often has good results. The pups produced from an outcross can vary widely in size and type. To fix the characteristic for which you have bred, choose the pup that most closely matches what you were going for and breed it back into your own line.

Only dogs that are outstanding examples of their breed and in the best of health should be used for breeding.

The Stud Agreement

There are as many ways to pay a stud fee as there are studs. The most important thing you can do is to make an agreement and put it in writing before the mating ever takes place.

Stud fees for Bloodhounds can range from as little as $300 to as much as $1,500. The amount of the fee depends on the stud's reputation, titles, and the quality of pups he has already produced. The stud owner may require that you put down a deposit or ask for the entire fee up front. Usually, if the bitch fails to conceive, she will receive an additional breeding at no charge. Some stud owners will also give a return breeding if the litter is very small or if all the pups are born dead.

In some cases, the stud owner may take a puppy as the stud fee. In this situation, the two of you need to agree ahead of time on what constitutes a litter. If only one puppy constitutes a litter, and that's all your bitch produces, you're out all your preparatory expenses, shipping costs, plus the stud fee, and you don't have a puppy. You may want to write into the contract that two puppies constitute a litter. Stud owners should also agree in advance on the sex of the puppy they will take.

Some stud owners charge by the number of registrable puppies. For instance, if your bitch produces ten puppies and three are mismarked or have kinked tails, you can choose not to register those three. The stud owner would then charge you the agreed-upon amount for each of the remaining registrable pups.

Shipping

When two dogs are bred, it is customary for the bitch to go to the dog. This may mean shipping her cross-country by air for a stay of a week or more. Be sure the stud owner has a copy of the bitch's flight itinerary if shipping is necessary. The stud fee may include the stud owner's time and expenses in picking up the bitch at the airport, her care and feeding while she is there, and taking her back to the airport for the return flight. Expect these expenses, which range from $100 to $150, to be nonrefundable.

Shipping can be stressful for Bloodhounds, especially if the weather is hot or if they must change planes. The stress of shipping can even affect the conception rate in females. If you can't find a direct nonstop flight or a direct flight where the dog doesn't have to change planes, you should think twice about shipping the dog unless you can go along and make sure she is transferred properly from one flight to another.

Artificial Insemination

If shipping is a problem, consider the use of artificial insemination. The use of fresh chilled semen or frozen semen has been very successful. It eliminates the hazards of shipping, and it makes a greater range of males available to your female.

Breeding Readiness

Bloodhound bitches go into estrus, or heat, twice a year. Usually, their first heat takes place when they are nine to twelve months old. Record the time, length, and other details of the first and subsequent heats so that you can see what kind of pattern develops: the length of time between heats, how long the heat lasts, and the signs your bitch displays. Most heats last 21 days. Your bitch may have a heavy flow of blood or show no signs at all. She may lick her vulva or urinate more frequently. And, of course, male dogs will show a greater interest in her.

When your bitch is at the proper age and has all her health clearances, you're ready to go. As soon as she goes into season, call the stud owner to make an appointment. Breeding usually takes place 10 to 14 days after the bitch goes into season.

The Mating Process

You might think this would be the easy part, but Bloodhounds often need a little help to complete the sexual act. Male Bloodhounds are notorious for their low libido, and inexperienced males may have no idea how to proceed. Your best bet is to match an inexperienced male with an experienced female.

Even so, because Bloodhounds are so large and have such pendulous body parts, human assistance may still be required to physically guide the dog and accomplish the mating. Some Bloodhounds are shy or fearful around other people, so if they need help, it's important that they be comfortable around strangers and with being handled and held. Once the tie takes place, it can last 30 to 45 minutes. The dogs are so big that some females may scream and flail, often for 20 or 30 minutes. If this is the case, you will need to help hold them together so they don't injure themselves.

Be sure the breeding area is escape-proof, free of distractions, and has nonskid flooring. Some items you might find helpful include a lubricant jelly, sterile latex gloves, and a muzzle. Usually, the bitch will be bred twice, two days apart, to ensure conception. The owner of the stud dog should record when matings take place and the details involved, such as the bitch's behavior and the length of the tie.

Hint. Schedule matings before meals so the dogs won't be sluggish. They'll also be less likely to suffer upset stomachs from the activity.

Care During the Pregnancy

Using the mating records, you can determine when Daisy should produce pups if she has become pregnant.

Signs of pregnancy include enlarged nipples, a slightly swollen vulva, increased appetite, and a cranky or demanding personality. At five weeks, she may begin to show. Ultrasound can confirm a pregnancy as early as 18 to 25 days. If ultrasound is unavailable, a blood test conducted at 25 to 37 days can indicate pregnancy.

Size of Litter

The average litter size for a Bloodhound bitch is eight pups, but it's not uncommon for her to be carrying 14 to 17 pups.

Exercise

Regular exercise during the pregnancy is essential for her to keep her muscle tone so she won't have problems delivering a large number of puppies. During the first part of the pregnancy, take her on plenty of long walks. As she gets heavier and larger, long walks won't be possible, but she should still have some physical exercise, even if it's just a couple of turns around the yard twice a day. Expect her to rest more often toward the end of the pregnancy.

Nutrition

Good nutrition is important as well. During the last six weeks of the pregnancy, feed a lactation or puppy diet that is high in protein. You need to make sure, however, that Daisy doesn't get too fat. Bloodhounds tend to be lazy whelpers, and excess weight can increase that tendency. Avoid giving bone meal or calcium supplements because these can increase the pups' likelihood of bloat or even cause a calcium deficiency in the bitch when she is nursing. Provide plenty of fresh water and clean, comfortable surroundings with no drafts or extreme temperatures. Keep Daisy clean, but avoid giving her a bath during the pregnancy to prevent the possibility of a chill or an injury in the tub to her or the unborn pups. During the pregnancy, Daisy should be sparkling with good health, displaying a shiny coat, clear eyes, and pink gums.

Medications

Certain treatments and medications should not be given during the pregnancy. Avoid flea-control products, deworming medications (heartworm preventive, however, should not be a problem; check with your veterinarian), and certain antibiotics. If Daisy becomes ill, be sure the veterinarian knows she is pregnant so he or she can tailor the treatment to her condition.

Gestation Period

The gestation period for dogs is 57 to 63 days. When whelping is imminent, Daisy's temperature will start to drop. Because you have kept accurate breeding records, you will have a good idea of when she is due to give birth, so for the last seven to ten days of gestation, you should take her temperature twice daily. When her temperature drops below 99°F (32.2°C), she will probably start whelping activity within 24 hours. Advise your veterinarian when whelping is imminent. If he or she won't be available, ask for a referral to another veterinarian, or be sure you know where the emergency clinic is. Oxytocin and calcium injections may be necessary to get the bitch through the pregnancy, and in a worst-case scenario she may need a Caesarean section for the last few puppies, which may or may not be alive.

Whelping

As the pups are born, Daisy should remove the placenta and sever the umbilical cord. If she's inexperienced, though, you may need to help her. The pups should remain in their placental sacs no longer than eight minutes, or their oxygen supply will be

Equipment to Keep on Hand for the Delivery

• whelping box (a sturdy, clean wood or something similar, with sides that are low enough so that the mother will not injure herself getting out of it but high enough so that the puppies cannot get out. Construct rails along inside walls of box, leaving enough room for pups to fit underneath. This prevents dam from rolling on them. Line the bottom of the box with washable towels or blankets.)
• rectal thermometer
• nasal aspirator
• scissors
• unwaxed dental floss
• iodine
• heating pad or heat lamp
• many towels and washcloths
• notepad and pen
• colored yarn or rickrack
• emergency phone numbers

depleted. Wipe out their nostrils and mouths to remove any mucus or fluids (use a nasal aspirator). Rub them briskly with a towel to stimulate circulation. Cut the umbilical cord about 2 inches (5.1 cm) from the abdomen

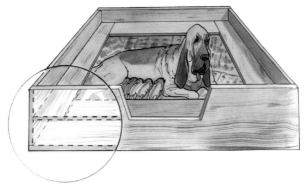

Rails on inside of box prevent dam from rolling on puppies.

and tie it with unwaxed dental floss. Dab the cut end with iodine to prevent infection. Keep a notepad and pen handy so you can jot down the time each puppy was born, whether it came with a placenta, and its weight at birth. Identify it with a piece of colored yarn or rickrack.

The labor of a Bloodhound bitch can go as long as 24 hours from first pup to last. Generally, the first six or eight puppies are delivered fairly easily, but after that the bitch may become tired and slow down. Some bitches lose their appetite just before labor, while others eat during labor. If labor is prolonged, it's important to get nutrition into the bitch to keep her strength up. If she won't eat, offer her some chicken broth or chicken broth mixed with Karo syrup. This provides salt, sugar, and fluids.

An extended labor means that the cervix is open for a long time, exposing the bitch to infections such as endometritis, or inflammation of the uterine lining. Another problem common to Bloodhounds is retained placentas, which can also cause infections. Be sure the number of placentas matches the number of pups. Call the veterinarian or take Daisy to the emergency hospital if her temperature goes up, she seems to be in extreme pain, she's shivering, trembling, or collapses, or if she has labored for more than three hours without producing a puppy.

Puppy Care

The First 48 Hours

Bloodhound mothers, especially first-timers, often have no idea how to care for their babies. Some are afraid of their puppies, while others have been known to roll over on them and crush them, or even to kill or eat the entire litter. Do not assume that these incidents are exceptions, and be prepared for anything. If the mother refuses to accept the pups, you will need to feed and care for them yourself.

Fearful mothers will sometimes come to accept their puppies after a day or two. You may need to force them to lie down in the box and accept the puppies for nursing. It is your responsibility to make sure that each pup is nursing and has a full stomach. The pups' intake of colostrum immediately after birth is crucial. Colostrum is the rich "first milk" and contains the maternal antibodies that help the pups fight off disease until they can be vaccinated. Some puppies may not be getting enough milk, either because they are ineffective nursers or because Daisy isn't producing enough. If you see a puppy that's not gaining weight and is crying because its stomach isn't full, you'll need to give it a supplement.

You also need to make sure the puppies are urinating and defecating. At this stage, the mother should lick the pups' urogenital areas to stimulate elimination, but if she doesn't you will need to take her place. Use a piece of cotton that has been dipped in warm water to simulate the mother's tongue, and wipe the pups' rears with an upward motion.

Even the best mothers have a hard time not lying on their puppies, even if they have litters of only five or six pups. To minimize the problem, be sure the whelping box is constructed with railings on the inside with enough room for pups underneath. Despite precautions, many Bloodhound mothers still manage to crush at least one puppy.

At this young age, puppies are unable to control their body temperature. The surrounding temperature should be 85°F (29°C) to prevent chills. Use a heating lamp or a well-insulated heating pad to help keep them warm.

A puppy is ready to go to its new home at 8 to 10 weeks of age, although some breeders like to keep them longer to ensure plenty of socialization. This Bloodhound is a good example of black and tan coloration.

HOW-TO:
Caring for Orphan Puppies

Sadly, the complications of whelping a big litter and the dangers of infection can sometimes end in the death of your bitch. In other instances, your bitch may refuse to have anything to do with her pups. Either way, you are left with the care of orphan puppies. For the first few weeks, they will need 'round-the-clock care, with frequent feedings, plenty of warmth and handling, and regular stimulation of elimination.

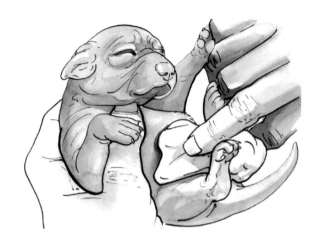

You'll have to take the dam's place in encouraging orphaned puppies to eliminate.

Feeding

There are formulas on the market that are made to replace bitch's milk. Goat's milk is another good substitute, and some breeders use homemade mixtures that contain evaporated milk, egg yolks, and yogurt. If you buy a commercial formula, the manufacturer will include information on the total volume the puppy should take in, based on its weight. Divide that total volume by six or eight feedings per day. As the puppies get older, they can go longer between meals.

Pups can be fed either with bottles or through a tube. Bottles are suitable if the pups have a good sucking reflex, but ineffective nursers tend to aspirate milk from the bottle, leading to the likelihood of pneumonia. Tube-feeding is more difficult and can be scary the first few times you do it, but sometimes it's the only way to get nutrition into the puppies.

Bottle-feeding. To bottle-feed, hold the pup with its stomach down and its head raised toward the nipple, just as if it were sucking at its mother's teat. This position reduces the possibility of the formula being sucked into the lungs. Let the puppy drink as much as it wants. When it is full, lay it on your lap and burp it by gently rubbing its back.

Tube-feeding. Your veterinarian should show you how to place the tube for tube-feeding. The risk you run with this method is accidentally feeding the tube down the trachea instead of the esophagus.

Bottle-feeding may be necessary for orphaned puppies.

Expect to use either method for the first two weeks. The pups can then be started on solid food.

Expect to see a steady weight gain. If the pups' stomachs should be full and they aren't crying or screaming, you're on the right track.

Elimination

After each meal, you'll need to stimulate urination and defecation. Puppies aren't capable of doing this on their own until they're about two weeks old. As described on page 69, moisten a cotton ball or small soft cloth with warm water. To stimulate urination, rub the genital area until a stream of urine appears. Repeat at the anus, wiping upward. Products made for babies, such as infant wipes, can also be used for this purpose.

Grooming

Keep the puppies wiped down and free of any fecal matter. Cleanse the face daily, especially around the eyes. This will help them as they start to open up.

Foster Care

Sometimes a substitute bitch can be found to nurse the pups, but because Bloodhounds are not common, this isn't something you should count on. Introduce the pups to her carefully, and watch for any signs of rejection.

Environment

Keeping the pups' body temperature at normal levels is crucial, especially for the first few days. Keep them in an environment where the temperature can be maintained at 90°F. A cozy whelping box with a heat lamp above it or a well-insulated heating pad can provide the warmth the puppies need. Make regular checks to ensure that the heat source is not too hot or too close to the pups. After the first four days, you can gradually reduce the temperature, first to 85°F, and, after a week, to 80°F. When the pups are 4 weeks old, the temperature can be reduced to 75°F.

To help your Bloodhound pups thrive, you'll need to provide the tactile stimulation they would have received from their mother. Stroke them gently with your fingers before feeding, and cuddle and pet them between meal times. Speaking or singing to them in a soft voice can be soothing as well.

Puppy Growth and Development

Puppies are born with their eyes and ears shut tightly against the world. They spend all their time eating and sleeping. Even as they sleep, however, they are growing rapidly, and you will see their tiny paws moving as if they are already on the trail. Any puppy that is not active in its sleep and not eating well is sick and should be seen by the veterinarian. Weigh the puppies daily. By the time they are 10 days old, their birth weight should have doubled. The eyes open anywhere from 7 to 14 days of age, and the ears become operative at 13 to 17 days. Baby teeth start to make an appearance around the third week.

As they grow, the pups' tiny teeth and nails will become sharp and annoying to their mother. Trim off the tips of the nails each week so they don't dig into her skin or injure each other, and soothe scratches with petroleum jelly.

For the first few weeks, Daisy will clean up after the pups by eating what they eliminate, but it won't be long before she teaches the pups to use one end of the whelping box as an elimination area. You should keep an eye on stool consistency and the pups' physical condition so you'll be alert to any problems. For instance, a red or swollen anus can indicate diarrhea. Keep the lining of the whelping box scrupulously clean, changing papers or towels regularly.

Feeding and Nutrition

Weaning time varies, but it usually begins at two to three weeks of age. Puppies can be started on solid food, usually a mixture of baby cereal and ground-up kibble, at about three weeks of age. Provide fresh water for the pups as well, in a heavy container that they can't overturn or fall into. If Daisy is a good mother and her pups are thriving, you can also let them continue to nurse until they are six or eight weeks old. Puppy kibble can be introduced at five or six weeks of age.

Bloodhound puppies grow rapidly. At birth, they weigh about 1 pound (.45 kg), although pups from larger litters may weigh less. Generally, for the first 8 to 12 weeks, they grow at least a pound a week. At 12 weeks they should be a minimum of 12 pounds (5.4 kg), and some puppies weigh up to 18 pounds (8 kg) at 12 weeks. By the time it is a year old, a male Bloodhound puppy will weigh about 90 pounds (41 kg). It's important not to accelerate that growth. Your puppy is going to gain 89 pounds (40 kg) during that first year, and it will achieve that weight whether it puts on the weight in the first three months or over the entire 12 months. Rapid growth accelerates the development of orthopedic problems and can make them worse. Puppies and young adults should not be allowed to get overweight, and they need a lot of free exercise. Ask your veterinarian about putting the puppy on an adult food when it is six months old.

Socialization

From day one, it's essential for Bloodhound puppies to become used to the scent, sound, and touch of humans. To prevent infection, you'll want to keep outside visitors away from the whelping area until the pups are several weeks old, but in the meantime you can handle and speak to them regularly—although not excessively—petting them and telling them what fine mantrailers, show dogs, and companions they will grow up to be. Most important, accustom the pups to all the sounds they will encounter out in the big world: kids playing, vacuum cleaners roaring, doorbells ringing, car doors slamming. A Bloodhound that is shy around people or fearful of sounds cannot fulfill its destiny.

At the same time, you must be sure Daisy is comfortable with people around her pups. Bitches can become territorial over their puppies, most commonly with strangers, but also with family members. The aggressive behavior she may develop during this time can last long after the pups are gone. If Daisy is primarily a family pet with a pleasant personality, this is something you should consider before deciding to breed her. The resulting change in her personality can be life-long.

The same is true of male Bloodhounds. Breeding a nice family pet can transfer his focus from you as his primary source of attention and affection. He may become more distracted, more territorial with other male dogs, and more dominant toward people, especially male people. This is why the decision to breed should be well thought out, not a one-time experience. That one time can forever shift the relationship you have with your dog.

Breeding your Bloodhound can change his or her personality and the way your dog acts toward other dogs and family members.

Health Care

The current trend in puppy immunizations is toward fewer vaccines given at a time. Some veterinarians believe there is a relationship between immune problems later in life and the bombardment of an immature immune system with modified-live vaccines. The first vaccinations are usually given at six weeks of age, or at least two weeks after the puppies are weaned. Some areas of the country have a higher incidence of parvo and distemper than others, and your veterinarian can advise you on the vaccination schedule that is appropriate for your area.

Your puppies will probably receive distemper and measles vaccinations at six weeks and a killed parvovirus vaccine at seven weeks. In areas where parvovirus is prevalent, a high-titer modified-live parvo vaccine is recommended. These vaccines can be given as early as four weeks of age in high-risk situations, such as your frequent attendance at other kennels, dog shows, and tracking trials, or if you work in a veterinary hospital or are in police work and come in contact with other dogs. Ideally, modified-live parvo vaccines are not given in combination with distemper vaccines. On the other hand, if you're in a relatively isolated area, Daisy is current on her vaccines, and you're not in contact with other dogs, the killed parvo vaccine is probably a better choice. A combination vaccine, particularly one that includes leptospirosis, probably won't be given until 12 weeks.

Most puppies are born carrying roundworms and should be dewormed at two weeks of age, and every two to three weeks thereafter until they are eight weeks old. Daisy should also be dewormed on this schedule, since she can pass the worms to the pups through her milk. If hookworms are a problem in your area, deworming can start at one week of age, continuing at two, four, six, and eight weeks. Good sanitation is the best way to keep worm populations down.

Record Keeping

Daisy and the stud dog must both be in compliance with AKC requirements for identification of dogs. This means they must have a tag, tattoo, or microchip that identifies them. After the puppies are born, you will need to write to the AKC for a litter registration packet. Fill in the information required and send the form to the owner of the stud dog for his or her signature. When the signed form is returned to you, it can be submitted to the AKC.

Finding New Homes

At eight to ten weeks of age, the pups are old enough to leave their mother and go to new homes. This is a wrenching time, but it will be easier if you have carefully interviewed prospective owners—just as you were interviewed when you bought your Bloodhound—and are confident they will give your pups the right kind of home.

Your responsibility to the pups does not end here. Having brought them into the world, you should be prepared to take them back at any time if their new homes don't work out. That's the bittersweet joy of being a breeder: sending fine young pups out into the world to make their way, but being willing to welcome them back home whenever times get hard.

Your Bloodhound's Health

A healthy Bloodhound is a joy to behold. It is tall and powerful with a short, thick coat. Its noble expression and sensitive temperament are characterized by deep-set "hound dog" eyes, long, droopy ears that are thin and soft to the touch, and folds of loose skin around the face. Bloodhound puppies are exuberant, and adults have a moderate activity level, something that may come as a surprise considering the stereotypical image of these dogs as lazy porch sleepers. And like most hounds, Bloodhounds love to eat. Given these attributes, it's easy for the observant owner to tell when a Bloodhound isn't feeling its best.

When to Call the Veterinarian

Lack of appetite and a low energy level are signs that your Bloodhound may need to visit the veterinarian. Other indications of health problems include weight gain or loss, excessive consumption of water, excessive urination, bad breath, bleeding gums, diarrhea or constipation, or a coat that is dry, dull, or flaky. For instance, appetite loss, bad breath, or bleeding gums can indicate dental problems; weight loss can signal parasite infestation; while obesity can be a sign of thyroid deficiency. A dog that drinks too much water and subsequently urinates excessively should be checked for diabetes or kidney disease. Poor coat condition may mean that a dog's food isn't providing the nutrients it needs, or that the dog is affected by internal parasites or a skin problem such as flea allergy dermatitis. Diarrhea is often a sign of intestinal problems or diseases such as parvovirus. By examining your Bloodhound on a weekly basis and keeping a diary of its condition, you can notice these types of changes and bring them to your veterinarian's attention before they become serious.

Health Concerns Specific to Bloodhounds

Gastric Torsion (Bloat)

In general, Bloodhounds are a healthy breed, but you should be aware of certain conditions to which they are prone. The most serious of these is gastric torsion, or bloat, which is common in large, deep-chested dogs. It occurs when the stomach twists, preventing the release of gas and fluids. Unless bloat is recognized and treatment—usually emergency surgery—initiated immediately, the dog could die.

A dog's chances of suffering bloat can be lessened through careful management of its diet and activity levels. This is accomplished by feeding two or more small meals daily rather than one large meal, raising food dishes off the floor, and limiting exercise and water consumption for two hours before and after the dog eats. For more information on bloat, see the section below under the Emergency Care heading, or contact the American Bloodhound Club, listed on page 92.

Hypothyroidism

Middle-aged or geriatric Bloodhounds may develop hypothyroidism, a common hormonal disorder in all dogs. Decreased thyroid function occurs when the thyroid gland is damaged or destroyed because of inflammation or cancer. Suspect hypothyroidism if your Bloodhound becomes lethargic, gains weight even though it isn't eating more, or develops a dull, dry coat. Sometimes large calluses form on the elbows and hocks of dogs with hypothyroidism. Hypothyroidism usually develops at five years or older.

Cardiomyopathy

Like other large and giant breeds, Bloodhounds have an increased incidence of cardiomyopathy, or enlargement of the heart. The cause of cardiomyopathy is unknown, but veterinary researchers suspect it is a genetic problem. If detected in its early stages, cardiomyopathy can be controlled with medication for a time.

Orthopedic Problems

Common inherited conditions in Bloodhounds include orthopedic problems such as hip dysplasia—a deformity of the hip joint—and various forms of elbow dysplasia, the most common of which is ununited anconeal process, which occurs when the elbow joint is incorrectly fused to the ulna, resulting in a fracture through the growth plate, which causes lameness. Other developmental degenerative joint diseases of the elbow that affect Bloodhounds are fragmented medial coronoid process and osteochondritis. Hip dysplasia can sometimes be controlled through diet and restricted activity, but in severe cases hip surgery or replacement is necessary. Surgery is required to repair ununited anconeal process.

Epilepsy

Epilepsy is also becoming more common in Bloodhounds. It is a seizure disorder caused by a temporary dysfunction of the brain. During a seizure, the dog's body may jerk or become rigid. It may or may not lose consciousness. Some dogs become anxious or excitable and may vocalize, drool, or lose control of their bladder and bowel function. Seizures appear disturbing, but in most cases they are not painful or life-threatening. There is no screening test for this disease, and because of its late onset in the breed, many Bloodhounds have already produced puppies before their epilepsy manifests itself. In mild cases, epilepsy can be controlled with medication.

Eye Problems

Inherited eye problems to which Bloodhounds may be subject are entropion, a condition in which the eyelids roll inward, and ectropion, in which the eyelids turn out. Entropion can damage the surface of the cornea and prevent tears from lubricating the cornea. Ectropion exposes the conjunctiva and cornea to irritation and

A Bloodhound in the peak of health is active, clear-eyed, has a shiny coat, and eats well.

injury. Both conditions usually require surgical correction.

Ear Infections

Because their ears are long and floppy, Bloodhounds can also be prone to ear infections. Suspect an ear infection if your Bloodhound frequently shakes or scratches at its head and ears, if the ears smell bad or are producing a discharge, or if the earflap or ear canal appear inflamed. Ear infections in Bloodhounds should be treated aggressively. Take your dog to the veterinarian as soon as you recognize a problem and continue treatment for double the usual amount of time. To prevent problems, keep the ears clean and dry.

Allergies

Finally, Bloodhounds can be sensitive to fleas and grass. Although allergies are not a huge problem in the breed, these sensitivities can be complicating factors in the development of skin and ear problems, as can yeast infections. To help prevent problems, keep your Bloodhound's ears food-free: Elevate its feeding dish and keep its ears out of the food by covering them with a snood. Don't forget to thoroughly wipe down your Bloodhound's lips, face, and ears after it eats. Remnants of food left on the skin can breed bacteria, causing infections.

Emergency Care

Good habits of observation and knowledge of first aid are vital for dog owners. In an emergency, veterinary help is a must, but sometimes a dog needs immediate care to save its life. Situations that require emergency first aid or quick recognition and response include:
- bleeding
- bloat
- broken bones
- burns

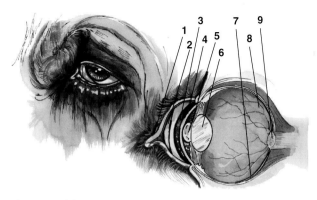

Anatomy of the eye.

1. medial canthus
2. third eyelid
3. iris
4. cornea
5. pupil
6. lens
7. retina
8. retinal vessels
9. optic disc

- choking
- frostbite
- heat exhaustion or heatstroke
- poisoning
- shock

By remaining calm and using the following techniques, you can stabilize your dog until you can get it to the veterinarian.

Bleeding

If a wound is gushing bright red blood, an artery is involved; the blood from a cut vein is dark red and has a more even flow. In either case, apply and maintain direct pressure with a gauze pad or other clean cloth. Secure the pad or have someone hold it in place, and seek veterinary help immediately.

Direct pressure is more effective than a tourniquet, and your dog's leg or tail can be damaged by a tourniquet used improperly. Use a tourniquet only if direct pressure fails to control the flow of blood. If a tourniquet is required, use a long piece of fabric such as a necktie, shoelace, or pantyhose. Place it directly above the wound, between the wound and the body, and tie a half knot. Then put a pencil or stick on top and complete the knot. You should be

1. nose
2. sinus cavity
3. brain
4. esophagus
5. trachea
6. spinal cord
7. thymus
8. lungs
9. heart
10. liver
11. diaphragm
12. stomach
13. spleen
14. kidney
15. jejunum
16. descending
    colon
17. ureter
18. bladder
19. anal sac

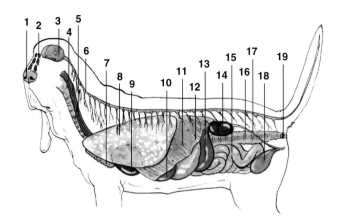

Internal organs of the Bloodhound.

able to fit a finger beneath the tourniquet when it is in place. Slowly twist the stick until the bleeding stops. To permit blood flow, release the tourniquet for a few seconds every five minutes. Then seek immediate veterinary help. If used incorrectly, tourniquets can do more harm than good, so use one *only* as a last resort.

If your dog's ear, foot pad, or penis is bleeding, take the injury seriously. Bleeding in these areas can be difficult to control. Apply pressure as described above and get the dog to a veterinarian.

Less serious bleeding, such as from a scratch or scrape, also requires treatment, although it is not life-threatening. Use three percent hydrogen peroxide to clean the wound. When the bleeding stops, apply antibiotic ointment. To ensure that there's no damage under the skin, you might ask your veterinarian to look at the wound.

Bloat

A Bloodhound in the early stages of bloat may pace restlessly or be lethar-gic. It may gag or make unsuccessful attempts to vomit, producing only excess saliva. Shallow breathing and a dull, vacant, or pained expression are other early indicators. The abdomen may appear distended, sounding hollow when thumped. If you are unsure whether the abdomen is expanding, use a cloth measuring tape to check abdominal size at the level of the last rib. Repeat the measurements frequently to see if the abdomen is growing in size. In later stages, the dog will retch or salivate, its pulse will weaken, its gums will grow pale, and it will be unable to stand. If you suspect bloat, do not wait to take the dog to the veterinarian, even if it's the middle of the night. The earlier bloat is caught, the more likely the dog is to survive.

Broken Bones

Broken bones can be caused by falls, run-ins with cars, or gunshot wounds. Any of these can happen to a Bloodhound simply because it is an active dog that spends a lot of time outdoors, generally not paying attention to anything but an interesting scent. The types of bone breaks include simple fractures and compound fractures. In the case of a compound fracture, the bone sticks out through the skin. If your dog breaks a bone, try to keep it as still as possible. A fracture can become more serious if the broken limb is moved too much. Wrap the dog in a blanket to help prevent shock, be sure it is cushioned during the car ride, and get to the veterinary hospital at once.

Shock

Shock is a common result of serious trauma. It is a potentially fatal condition in which the body is unable to maintain adequate blood pressure, meaning that the vital organs such as the brain, heart, and lungs don't get enough oxygen-rich blood and thus fail to function properly. If your dog has been hit by a car or suffered some other trauma, it may go into shock. Blood loss, poisoning, or severe fluid loss from vomiting or diarrhea can also cause a dog to go into shock. Shock is indicated by a weak, rapid pulse, dry gums and lips that are pale or gray, shallow, rapid breathing, a low body temperature, and weakness or lethargy. Control any bleeding, keep the dog still and warm, and seek immediate veterinary treatment.

Spinal Injuries

A dog that is hit by a car may suffer spinal injuries. This may be the case if your dog is paralyzed, its legs are rigid, stiff, or limp, or its head is thrust backward. If you suspect a spinal injury, move your dog as little and as carefully as possible. Improvise a stretcher using a board large enough to support the dog's back. Tape or otherwise secure the dog to the board so it won't roll off or move around. If a board is not available, you can use a blanket pulled taut. If possible, have

someone help you slide the dog onto the stretcher instead of lifting it. Treat the dog for shock as needed, and try to keep it as still as possible during the ride to the veterinary hospital. Your dog will no doubt be frightened and in pain, so offer plenty of verbal reassurance.

Fractured Jaw or Skull

If your dog's lower jaw is hanging open and it is drooling, the jaw may be fractured. Tie a bandage or scarf underneath the chin, fastening it behind the ears, and get to a veterinarian. A dizzy or unconscious dog, or one with a bloody nose, may have a skull fracture. Gently control any bleeding and seek veterinary help immediately.

Burns

A burn to your dog's paws or fur should be bathed with cool water or treated with a cool compress. *Use cool water only, never ice, butter, or ointment of any kind.* Ice can damage the skin, and butter and ointments merely hold the heat in. If a large area of the dog's body is burned, cover that area with a thick layer of gauze or cloth (cotton balls or cotton batting will

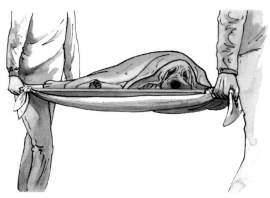

You may have to improvise a stretcher for a badly injured dog.

The average lifespan of a Bloodhound is 8 to 10 years.

hands by wearing rubber gloves. Seek immediate veterinary treatment.

Puppies and adolescent dogs are likely to chew on electrical cords, leading to the possibility of electrical burns on the corners of the mouth or on the tongue and palate. In the case of electrical shock, the dog may convulse or lose consciousness, its respiration may slow, and severe shock may cause the heart to stop beating. If you find your dog in this condition, don't touch it until you switch off the electrical source. Then get it to a veterinarian right away. If you know how to perform CPR on your pet, do not initiate it unless you are sure the heart has stopped. Otherwise, you could cause more damage. See box.

Choking

With their powerful noses, Bloodhounds are always investigating, and ingesting items is a large part of a dog's investigative process. Bloodhounds are particularly likely to try to eat foreign objects. Bones, rocks, small balls, and tinsel are just a few of the things a Bloodhound might swallow that could cause it to choke. Any time you see your dog coughing, gagging, or pawing at its mouth, check for an obstruction. Open the mouth by pressing your thumb and forefingers into the upper cheeks. Gently try to remove the obstruction with your fingers or a pair of needle-nose pliers. If you can't remove the object, perform the Heimlich maneuver by standing behind the dog, encircling its abdomen with your arms just beneath or behind the rib cage, and compressing the chest. Repeat until the object is coughed up. If you can't remove it, get the dog to a veterinarian immediately.

Frostbite

Dogs in less than peak condition—those that are very young, very old, or sick—are most prone to frostbite, a

stick to the damaged skin), keep the dog warm to prevent shock, and get it to a veterinarian immediately.

Substances such as battery acid or some toilet bowl cleaners can cause chemical burns. These burns can be treated in the same manner as other burns, but be sure to protect your

Performing CPR

CPR stands for cardiopulmonary resuscitation and should be performed only when your dog is not breathing and has no pulse. CPR doesn't always work, but it can give your dog an extra chance. To perform CPR, lay your dog on its side on a flat, hard surface. Using the flat of your hand, apply pressure directly over the heart (behind the front legs in the lower half of the chest), repeating compressions about 120 times per minute. After each three compressions, give two artificial breaths. If CPR is not successful after five or 10 minutes, it's best to stop trying.

painful condition that results from prolonged exposure to very cold temperatures. The areas likely to be affected are the footpads, tail, and ear tips. Frostbite is indicated by skin that becomes pale, then reddens and becomes hot and painful to the touch, swelling, and peeling of external skin layers. Keep the frostbitten dog warm, but thaw frostbitten areas slowly. Massaging the skin or applying hot compresses can worsen the damage; instead, apply warm, moist towels and change them frequently. When the skin regains its normal color, stop warming it. Wrap the dog in a blanket to help prevent shock, and get it to a veterinarian right away.

Heat Exhaustion and Heatstroke

Dogs have few sweat glands that perform a cooling function, so they must control their body temperature by panting. As the dog pants, body heat is lost by evaporation from the mouth. If the dog is unable to disperse heat quickly enough, its body temperature can rise to a dangerous level. Dogs can easily become overheated if left in a car on a hot day or in other situations where the environmental temperature is high. Heat exhaustion is associated with excessive exercise on hot days, but the dog's temperature doesn't necessarily rise to dangerous levels. A dog with heat exhaustion may collapse, vomit, or have muscle cramps. Heatstroke can develop in only a few minutes, the body temperature rising to 108°F (42.2°C) or higher. A dog with heatstroke can die if it is not immediately cooled and taken to a veterinarian. Wet the dog's body with cool—not cold—water, and get it to a veterinarian.

Poisoning

Household cleansers, rat poisons, and yard treatments can all cause internal or external poisoning in dogs, especially in curious breeds such as Bloodhounds. Also toxic are seasonal plants such as Easter lilies, common household, yard, and garden plants such as azaleas, caladium, Dieffenbachia (dumbcane), English ivy (berries and leaves), ficus (leaves), holly, mistletoe (berries), oleander, and philodendron, and bulbs such as amaryllis, daffodil, iris, and tulip. Indications that your dog has come into contact with something poisonous include drooling, vomiting, convulsing, muscle weakness, diarrhea, or collapse. Sometimes the eyes, mouth, or skin become irritated.

Rapid, expert advice is vital. If veterinary care is not immediately available but you can identify the substance, call the National Animal Poison Control Center for advice. The phone number for the NAPCC is listed on page 92. If the poison is external, put on rubber gloves and wash the affected area with warm water. If you believe the dog has been poisoned by something it ate, give activated charcoal tablets to help adsorb the poison, binding it to the surface of the charcoal so it doesn't spread through the bloodstream. Do not induce vomiting unless advised to by the NAPCC or your veterinarian. Take the dog to your veterinarian as soon as possible. Be sure to bring the package containing the suspected poison and a sample of anything your dog has vomited.

Puncture Wounds

This type of wound can be caused by a bite or by a sharp object entering the dog's paw or other area of the body. If not treated properly, a puncture wound can become infected or abscessed. Signs of infection include swelling, redness, warmth, and pain. Sometimes, pus collects in the wound, causing an abscess to form.

Cleanse a bite or puncture wound by flushing the area with a mild disinfectant such as 0.0001 percent povidone-iodine or 0.05 percent chlorhexidine. It's a good idea to take your dog to the veterinarian within 24 hours for a course of antibiotics, especially with bite wounds, which become infected easily. Your veterinarian probably won't stitch up a bite wound because the area will need to drain if it becomes infected.

The First Aid Kit

Ready-made pet first aid kits are available, but you can also assemble one yourself from common household items. Tape or write your veterinarian's phone number in the box where you keep the supplies, as well as the phone number of and directions to the nearest emergency clinic. Be sure the first aid kit is identified as such and store it in an easily accessible area. With luck, you won't ever have to use your kit, but if you do, remember to replace items when you run low. The following items are part of a well-stocked first aid kit:
• activated charcoal (available at drug stores) for adsorbing poisons
• adhesive tape to secure bandages
• antibacterial ointment or powder for cleaning wounds
• blunt-tipped scissors to trim hair from wounds and cut bandaging material

• cotton balls
• cotton swabs
• disinfectant solution
• eye dropper, turkey baster, or syringe to flush wounds
• gauze pads and rolls to make bandages
• 3 percent hydrogen peroxide to clean wounds or induce vomiting as instructed by veterinarian
• Kaopectate (ask your veterinarian what amount is appropriate to control your dog's diarrhea)
• K-Y jelly or petroleum jelly to lubricate a thermometer
• Needleless syringe for giving liquid medications
• Needle-nose pliers to remove obstructions from the mouth or throat
• Plaster splint for broken limbs
• Rectal thermometer
• Sanitary napkins to help stem blood flow
• Syrup of ipecac to induce vomiting as instructed
• Towels
• Tweezers

Giving Medication

At some point in its life, it is likely that your Bloodhound will require some form of medical care at home. Knowing how to give a pill, administer liquid medications, or place eye and ear drops is an important adjunct to regular veterinary care, ensuring that the home care your Bloodhound receives will support the treatment prescribed by the veterinarian. By learning how to give a pill or take your dog's temperature, you will be less likely to panic if it becomes ill, and it will be more amenable to receiving the medication and treatment it needs.

Each dog is an individual, and many factors affect how well a medication will work. These include age and condition. Very young or very old dogs may respond differently to medications than adolescent or middle-aged dogs,

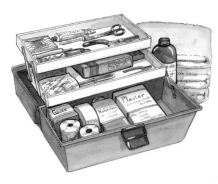

Keep an emergency first aid kit well stocked and handy.

and the same holds true for dogs that are over- or underweight. A drug's effectiveness can also be affected by when it is given. Some medications must be given on a full stomach, but other drugs are neutralized by food. Often, medications must be taken in a certain sequence or in concert with other drugs. The method and frequency of administration are also important. Ask your veterinarian to confirm how frequently the medication should be given and whether the medication should be administered orally (by mouth) or topically (on the skin). Ask for written instructions if the medication procedure seems complicated. Heat can spoil a medication's effectiveness, so don't let bottles or tubes sit out in the sun.

The next step is to actually get the medication into your dog. The more skilled you are, the easier it will be. Remain calm and patient, and the whole thing will be less stressful for both of you. A treat or praise afterward may help your dog view medicine time as more pleasant.

Giving Pills

Some lucky pet owners have dogs that will eat pills mixed with their food. If this is not the case in your household, or if your dog has lost its appetite, the following techniques will help you get pills into your dog.

With the pill in your right hand, gently open the dog's jaws with your left first and middle fingers. Place the pill far back on the tongue, then close the mouth and hold it closed while stroking the throat. Another technique that works well is to hold the dog's head in your left hand. Tip the head back until the dog is looking straight up. Holding the pill between the thumb and forefinger of your right hand, open the mouth with the middle finger of your right hand. Drop the pill into the back of the mouth and push it over the tongue with the index finger of your right hand. Close the mouth and blow into your dog's nose to make it lick, thus inducing swallowing. If you are left-handed, just reverse these directions. Some pills have an unpleasant flavor if they are broken, so try to give a whole pill whenever possible.

If the above methods don't work, disguise the pill by wrapping it in a tempting treat such as cream cheese, liver sausage, or peanut butter. Unless your Bloodhound is extremely picky, it won't even realize the pill is there. Be sure to check with your veterinarian to make sure this method won't affect the pill's efficacy.

Bloodhounds can be tricky; they have been known to hold pills in their mouths and spit them out when no one's looking. It's important to have an effective pill-giving technique so the dog receives the entire amount prescribed at the appropriate times each day. Even if your dog appears to be well, continue giving the medication until it is all gone. Your veterinarian prescribed that amount for a reason, so don't try to second-guess him or her.

Liquids

Fill a medicine dropper or syringe with the appropriate amount of medication. Restrain your Bloodhound as described above. Tilting the head upward, open the mouth and aim the dropper at the cheek pouch. Holding the mouth closed around the dropper, squeeze out the medication. The automatic swallowing reflex will kick in as the liquid reaches the back of the mouth. Another good way to induce swallowing is by blowing into the Bloodhound's nose to make it lick.

Ear Drops

Putting drops into a Bloodhound's floppy ears can be difficult. A shake of the head is likely to send the drops flying through the air. To avoid this, tilt

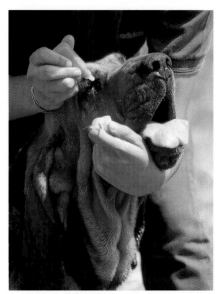

Teach your Bloodhound when it is young to accept being handled. This will make it easier to apply eye drops and ointments and give other medications.

the head slightly to the opposite side. Administer the required amount of medication; then gently hold the ear flap closed and massage the cartilage at the base of the ear. The massaging action gets the medication into the ear, ensuring that less of it is lost if the dog shakes its head. This massage will feel good to your Bloodhound unless its ears are unusually painful.

Eye Drops

Hold your Bloodhound's head firmly so it doesn't shake it, causing you to poke it in the eye. With the eye drops in your right hand (reverse this if you are left-handed), tilt the head upward and place the drops in the inner corner of the eye, directly on the eyeball. Avoid touching the eye with the tip of the applicator. Close and open the eyelids to ensure that the medication is distributed evenly.

Ointments

Ointments generally are applied to a dog's eyes or ears. To medicate eyes, hold the dog's head firmly. Gently pull down on the lower lid, exposing the inner eyelid. Apply the ointment to the inside lower lid, avoiding direct application to the eyeball. You may also pull back the upper lid and place the ointment on the white of the eye. Then close the dog's eyelids to distribute the medication. To apply ointments to ears, follow the directions for ear drops.

Flea Control

Although not strictly medications, flea control products contain chemicals that can affect your dog's health. Use these products with care and follow the directions on the label. Just as with medications, age can be a factor. Note whether the product is safe for puppies and old dogs. If you are treating both your home and your dog for fleas, avoid mixing types of products except under veterinary supervision, as some chemicals when mixed can have a toxic effect. Early signs of chemical poisoning include excessive salivation and nervous tremors, followed by collapse, convulsions, and coma. Manufacturers of flea-control products have worked hard to develop safe, effective methods of control, and to a large extent they have succeeded. Several new products are available that are toxic only to fleas, not to dogs (see page 86). Ask your veterinarian to advise you about which of these flea-fighting methods is best for your situation.

Human Medications

There are some instances in which your veterinarian may recommend giving a medication common in human use, such as Dramamine for carsickness, hydrogen peroxide to induce vomiting, and Kaopectate for diarrhea. Give these drugs to your dog only under veterinary supervision, and ask your veterinarian what dosage is correct for your dog. *Never give medications of any type without first asking your veterinarian's advice.*

Taking Your Dog's Temperature

You may need to take your dog's temperature if you suspect heatstroke or infection. Normally, a dog's temperature ranges from 100°F (37.8°C) to 102.5°F (39°C), with the danger level at 106°F (41°C) or higher. To take your dog's temperature, lubricate a rectal thermometer with petroleum jelly, K-Y jelly, or vegetable oil, and gently insert the thermometer into the rectum. For safety, use a digital rather than a glass thermometer. Sometimes it's helpful to have someone else hold the dog while you insert the thermometer. Remove the thermometer after one minute. Call your veterinarian if the dog's temperature is nearing or above the danger level, or if the temperature increases throughout the day or on consecutive days.

External Parasites

Fleas, ticks, and mites are all external parasites that can affect your Bloodhound. A parasite is an organism that makes its living off other life forms. Fleas and ticks, for instance, get their sustenance by sucking the blood of their victims. Parasites can spread disease and even play a role in the transmission of other parasites, such as tapeworms, to your dog. Keeping your Bloodhound free of parasites is an important part of its overall good health.

Fleas

Fleas are a dog's most common and annoying external parasite. Unless you live in a hot, dry climate or a very cold climate, your dog is likely to suffer from the constant itching caused by the bites of these pests.

The bite of a single flea can cause sensitive dogs to chew and scratch at the ferocious itch.

Some dogs are so sensitive to flea saliva—the substance that causes the itch—that a single bite can send them into a frenzy of scratching and biting at the sensitive area. These dogs suffer from a condition called flea allergy dermatitis, which manifests itself in severe itching, crusty sores on the dog's body, and thickening of the skin. Bacterial skin infections are often a secondary response.

Fortunately, Bloodhounds have short coats, so it's easier to find fleas on them than it is on longhaired breeds. To determine if your Bloodhound is infested with fleas, run a fine-toothed flea comb through its coat. Even if you find only one or two fleas, it's evidence that there are probably a lot more biding their time in your house. Another way to scout out fleas is to brush your dog while it's standing over a white cloth or piece of paper. If small black flecks fall onto the white area, moisten them to see if they turn red. When this happens, what you've discovered is flea dirt, or the blood excreted by the flea after it has fed on your dog.

Flea Control

There are many good flea control products on the market. The newest ones are harmful only to fleas, not to dogs, putting the fleas out of commission by attacking their nervous systems or reproductive abilities. Ask your veterinarian to help you determine the best product for your Bloodhound, based on the climate in your area and your dog's lifestyle. A dog that spends a lot of time outdoors on the trail or splashing through water may need a different regimen than one that is primarily a house or show dog.

To keep these pesky bloodsuckers at bay requires a three-pronged program of treating the dog, the indoor environment, and the outdoor environment. The vacuum cleaner and the washing machine will be your best friends in this process.

When you discover a flea infestation, the first thing to do is to develop a battle plan. You'll need to purchase the appropriate flea-control products, set aside time to apply them to the dog, the household premises and the yard, vacuum the house, and launder the pet bedding as well as your own, using hot water. Don't forget to treat the doghouse and the interior of your car. Be sure to check with your veterinarian to confirm that the products you're using aren't harmful in combination with each other.

Vacuuming. During flea season, the first rule is to vacuum early and vacuum often. Fleas and their eggs thrive in carpeted areas, so frequent vacuuming is needed to suck them out of their hideaways. You might also consider having the carpet professionally cleaned and then applying a nontoxic powder that contains borax—which kills fleas by drying them out—to the carpet and furniture. Such powders are very effective and often are guaranteed for up to one year. They can be professionally applied or you can purchase them at pet stores and do it yourself.

Flea bombs and sprays. A serious infestation of fleas may require the use of a flea "bomb." Of course, you and all your pets will need to be out of the house for several hours while the bomb works. For a milder infestation, regular application of a premise spray around the baseboards and underneath furniture may be all that is needed. Never use a premise or yard spray on your dog. Flea control products are specially formulated for specific uses, which will be spelled out in the directions.

The yard. Finally, flea control is also necessary for the yard. It's probably not possible to treat the whole yard, unless you hire a professional exterminator, so your best bet is to spray around the fence line, around the house, and under and around decks. Keep debris picked up so fleas will have fewer choice places to lay their eggs. If you do choose to hire an exterminator, be sure to ask about the safety for pets of the product used. Double-check with your veterinarian before you allow the yard to be treated.

There are a number of different types of flea-control products. Generally, the least toxic are those containing pyrethrins or pyrethroids. Pyrethrins are derived from the chrysanthemum plant; pyrethroids are synthetic versions of pyrethrins. A pyrethrin product usually works quickly but doesn't stay long in the environment.

More powerful and long-lasting chemicals are found in such products as dips, flea collars, and yard sprays. These chemicals, which are cholinesterase inhibitors, go by the names Carbaryl, Diazinon, Dursban, Fenthion, Malathion, and Sevin. They should be used sparingly on and around dogs; more is not better.

Recent developments in flea control include insect growth regulators, or IGRs, which prevent flea larvae from reaching adulthood, and systemic products (pills and topical applications) that are harmful only to the flea, not to the dog. Thanks to these advances, flea control is safer and more successful than ever. However, it's still important to note that before using any flea-control product, you should always read the directions carefully and follow them to the letter.

Ticks

Ticks are members of the arachnid family. They have tear-shaped bodies with eight legs and generally are brown or black. An adult female tick is about the size of a sesame seed. While not as common as fleas, ticks can pose more serious problems. Using their sharp mouthpieces, ticks attach themselves to a dog's skin, most commonly around the head, neck, ears, or feet. A large number of ticks feeding off a single dog can cause severe anemia or tick paralysis, and ticks transmit Lyme disease and Rocky Mountain spotted fever. The two ticks most commonly found on dogs are the brown dog tick and the American dog tick, but the deer tick and the western black-legged tick, both of which transmit Lyme disease, also feed on dogs.

Spring and summer are when ticks are out in full force. Any time your Bloodhound is outdoors, especially if it's in a heavily wooded area, you should examine it for ticks. Wearing gloves, carefully part the fur and look down close to the skin. Unless they're already bloated with blood, ticks can be easy to miss, especially on dogs with dark coats.

To remove ticks, use tweezers or forceps to grasp the tick at its head. Pull the tick out slowly yet firmly so you don't leave any part of it behind. Spraying the tick with a flea-and-tick insecticide before removal can help loosen the tick's grasp. Never try to burn the tick off; you'll only succeed in injuring your dog. Other methods that should be avoided are covering the tick with nail polish, petroleum jelly, kerosene, or gasoline. Be sure you don't touch the tick with your bare hands. The spirochete that causes Lyme disease can enter through breaks in your skin.

Many products are available that will help kill or repel ticks, and your dog can be vaccinated for Lyme disease if your veterinarian thinks the risk of infection warrants it. Usually, the vaccine is recommended if there is a high incidence of Lyme disease in the area in which you live or if the dog's lifestyle puts it at risk. For instance, a mantrailing Bloodhound that works frequently in the forests of northern Michigan would be much more likely to require vaccination than one working in New Mexico, a state that has few if any cases of Lyme disease.

Mites

Like ticks, mites are also arachnids. Four species of mites can infest dogs: *Demodex canis,* which causes canine demodicosis, sometimes known as demodectic mange; *Sarcoptes scabei* var. *canis,* which causes canine scabies, also known as sarcoptic mange; *Cheyletiella,* which causes a mild, itchy skin disease; and *Otodectes cynotis,* or ear mites.

Demodicosis. The cigar-shaped *Demodex* mites commonly live in harmony with dogs, inhabiting the hair follicles of the skin, but sometimes their population gets out of control. That's when demodicosis develops. Demodicosis, which is not contagious, can be localized, occurring only in a single area, or it can become generalized, spreading over the entire body. Fortunately, the much milder localized demodicosis is more common. Demodicosis is more likely to develop in young dogs less than a year old, but adults can also acquire it. There's a strong likelihood that juvenile-onset

Bloodhounds are pack animals that enjoy the company of their own kind and of their people.

demodicosis is hereditary in nature. Young dogs that develop it should be spayed or neutered.

Signs of demodicosis are patchy hair loss and reddened, scaly skin, especially around the face, eyes, corners of the mouth, and on the front legs. In generalized demodicosis, these signs are more severe and more widespread, and the skin may become darker and thicker because of chronic inflammation. The feet can also be severely affected. The presence of *Demodex* mites is confirmed by skin scrapings or sometimes skin biopsies.

Localized demodicosis usually goes away on its own. If necessary, your veterinarian can prescribe an ointment that will kill the mites. More drastic treatment is required for generalized demodicosis. Usually, the dog's entire coat must be clipped and the dog dipped once or twice weekly in a solution to kill the mites. Antibiotics will be prescribed for the secondary infections. In some cases the dog may

need whirlpool soaks and frequent baths with a shampoo containing benzoyl-peroxide. Even with all this, the dog's recovery is not guaranteed, especially if it is getting on in years.

Canine scabies. Unlike demodicosis, canine scabies is highly contagious between dogs and sometimes to people and cats. This skin disease occurs when the small oval white *Sarcoptes* mite burrows under the dog's skin, causing intense itching. Signs of scabies are itching, crusty sores, hair loss, and the injuries caused by the dog biting and scratching at the itchy spots. These signs, plus skin scrapings, can help your veterinarian diagnose this parasite.

A dog with scabies should be separated from other members of the household. Your veterinarian will prescribe shampoos and dips to kill the mites. Usually, at least six dips, one every five days, are necessary. To help control the itching, the veterinarian may prescribe corticosteroids. Any other pets that have had frequent contact with the infested dog should also be treated, whether or not they show signs.

Cheyletiella mites. Infestation with *Cheyletiella* mites is not common, especially if a good flea-control program is in place. The condition caused by these mites is a mild but contagious itchy skin disease that can be transmitted to other animals and to people. It occurs most often in puppies and adolescent dogs.

Cheyletiella mites, which look like small white specks, can be seen with the naked eye on the dog's skin or fur. Signs of infestation are dandruff along the dog's back and sometimes mild itching. A skin scraping can confirm the presence of the mites. Like other mite infestations, treatment involves a series of medicated baths and dips. Other dogs and cats in the household that have been exposed should also be treated and the house thoroughly cleaned to make sure no mites remain.

Ear mites. Ear mites make their home in an animal's ear canal. They prefer cats, but dogs are not immune. Suspect ear mites if your Bloodhound has dry, reddish-brown or black ear wax and frequently shakes its head or paws at its ears. If you remove some of the wax and examine it closely, you may be able to see the tiny—no larger than a pinpoint—white mites moving around.

A severe infestation of ear mites can stop up the whole ear canal and lead to serious yeast or bacterial infections. If ear mites are diagnosed, your veterinarian will prescribe a solution to be placed in the ear that will kill the mites. Treatment must continue for at least 30 days to ensure that all the mites are killed. It's also a good idea to bathe the dog, just in case any mites escape from the ear.

Internal Parasites

The most common internal parasites that affect dogs are roundworms, hookworms, whipworms, tapeworms, and heartworms. Internal parasites are a serious problem because, among other things, they can consume nutrients a dog needs or prevent the dog's body from properly absorbing those nutrients, destroy red blood cells, causing anemia, damage or kill tissues and cells as they move through the body, and transmit disease. If the infection is severe, some internal parasites, such as heartworms, can even kill a dog.

Roundworms

Most dogs have been infected with roundworms *(Toxocara canis)* at one time or another in their lives, most likely at birth. Even if the mother was dewormed during pregnancy, she can still transmit roundworms through her milk. In adult dogs, roundworms

rarely cause serious problems, but puppies can be severely affected and may even die from a heavy load of roundworms.

A puppy with a bellyful of worms is thin and scrawny, except for a pot-belly, and its coat is rough and dull. Vomiting and diarrhea are common signs of roundworm infection, and the puppy may have a cough or even develop pneumonia. Avoid buying a Bloodhound puppy with these signs. If it's too late and you've already acquired such a pup, take it to your veterinarian for treatment with a dewormer. Whether or not they show signs of infection, puppies should be dewormed every two weeks until they are eight weeks old, according to recommendations by the Centers for Disease Control.

Roundworm transmission to people is rare, but young children can acquire them by touching egg-laden feces or playing in dirt or grassy areas where roundworm eggs have been deposited, and then putting their hands in their mouths. Roundworm infection can be prevented by keeping the yard clean of feces, which should be picked up daily. Adult dogs should have an annual fecal exam so they can be treated for any worms that may be present.

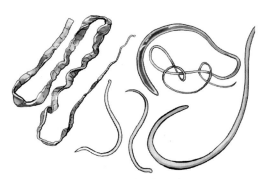

Tapeworm, whipworm, roundworm, and hookworm.

Hookworms

Bloodhounds that live in the southern United States or any other area with a warm, humid climate are more likely to fall victim to hookworms than Bloodhounds in dry climates. Hookworms can penetrate the skin, usually through the feet, or they can be transmitted to pups through their mother's milk. Once they migrate through the body to the small intestine, hookworms latch onto the intestinal wall and suck blood from it, causing anemia in severe cases. Diarrhea, weakness, and weight loss are other signs of hookworm infection. To confirm an invasion of hookworms, your veterinarian will need to examine a stool sample for hookworm eggs. Medication can be given to kill the worms, but unless feces are picked up often, infection will recur quickly.

Whipworms

Like hookworms, whipworms (Trichuris vulpis) feed on blood, but they live in the large intestine. They are transmitted when the dog eats something that has been in contact with contaminated soil or infective larvae. Mild infections usually don't cause a problem, but anemia, diarrhea, and weight loss can occur when too many whipworms inhabit the dog. Because their eggs are passed only occasionally, whipworms can be difficult to diagnose, and it may take several fecal exams before their presence is confirmed. As with other internal parasites, there are drugs that will kill the worms, but only a regular yard clean-up program will prevent reinfection.

Tapeworms

Tapeworms look like long, flat ribbons. They have hooks or suckers on their heads, which they use to attach themselves to their host. The most common type of tapeworm found in dogs is called *dipylidium caninum,* which is spread by fleas. Fortunately, it's pretty harmless, causing only disgust when you find white, ricelike segments of it crawling on your dog's rear end or in its bedding or stool. Your veterinarian can prescribe medication to get rid of the tapeworms, and good flea-control measures will help keep them away.

Heartworms

It used to be that only Bloodhounds living in the warm, humid climate of the southern United States needed to worry about heartworm infection, but these killers have now spread throughout the country. Transmitted by the bite of a mosquito, heartworm larvae develop in subcutaneous tissues and then enter the bloodstream, which carries them to the pulmonary arteries and the right side of the dog's heart, where they reach maturity and produce young called microfilariae. When a mosquito bites the dog, it ingests the microfilariae, which go through a developmental stage in the mosquito's body and are then deposited through the mosquito bite

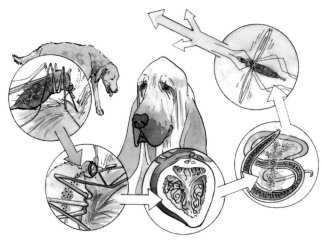

The life cycle of the heartworm.

into a dog's bloodstream, beginning the life cycle all over again.

When adult heartworms become numerous enough, they can cause such signs as lack of energy, weight loss, coughing after exertion, and eventually congestive heart failure. Diagnosis requires a blood test and sometimes X rays. Treatment takes six weeks or more and requires administration of drugs that are dangerous not only to the heartworms but also to the dog.

Heartworm infection is easily prevented with medications that can be given either daily or monthly, depending on your preference. Some heartworm medications also kill roundworms and hookworms.

Your Aging Bloodhound

A Bloodhound usually lives eight to ten years with good care, with a few lasting as long as twelve to fourteen years. Unneutered males tend to have the shortest lifespan; spayed females the longest. As your Bloodhound's years increase, it will become less active but still capable of enjoying life, albeit as an observer rather than a participant. To ensure your Bloodhound a long, healthy life span, start when it is a puppy by providing a complete, balanced diet and regular veterinary care. When it starts getting on in years, at about age five, take it to the veterinarian for a geriatric exam. The examination and tests your veterinarian performs will help establish a baseline of good health, against which the dog can be judged as it grows older. Such an exam can also catch problems in their early stages, while they are still treatable. Common problems in aging Bloodhounds include hypothyroidism and dry eye. In addition, you can take some simple steps to make life easier for your aging Bloodhound:
• Be sure it has a comfortable bed in a warm place. Its bones are a little

achier now, so anything you can do to ease its joints will be appreciated.
• Take it out to eliminate more often. Very young puppies and old dogs don't have the holding capacity of dogs in their prime. Save your carpet and your Bloodhound's dignity by ensuring that the dog has plenty of opportunities to eliminate outdoors. If extra trips during the day aren't possible due to your work schedule, put down papers so it has an acceptable place to go.
• Keep up the exercise. Although it's probably no longer capable of tracking for miles, it will still enjoy a walk, with plenty of opportunities to sniff the scent messages left by canine pals.
• Schedule an annual dental cleaning. Periodontal disease can make your dog's teeth ache, and it will be less inclined to eat if its mouth hurts. Regular brushing, plus a thorough veterinary cleaning, will keep teeth and gums in good shape and prevent the development of bacterial infections that can spread throughout the body.

The End of a Life

As everything must, even a beloved Bloodhound's life comes to an end. When your dog is very old and no longer enjoying life—refusing to eat and incapable of going for the walks that once meant so much—it is time to talk to your veterinarian about euthanasia. The greatest gift you can give your dog is a peaceful, pain-free death. A caring veterinarian will permit you to stay with your dog while the injection is given, a last chance to say how much you love it.

Afterward, feel no shame in grieving. The love of a dog is precious and not to be trivialized. It may comfort you to make a donation in its memory to canine health research or to an animal welfare organization. Then it will be time to start thinking about bringing another Bloodhound into your life.

Useful Addresses and Literature

Organizations

American Bloodhound Club
Ed Kilby, Secretary
1914 Berry Lane
Daytona Beach, FL 32124*

American Kennel Club
5580 Centerview Drive, Suite 200
Raleigh, NC 27606-3390
(919) 233-3600

Canine Eye Registration Foundation
South Campus Court, Building C
West Lafayette, IN 47907

National Animal Poison Control
Center (900) 680-0000 ($20 for
five minutes and $2.95 per minute
thereafter); (888) 4ANIHELP or
(800) 548-2423 ($30 per case, credit
card only)

National Police Bloodhound
Association (see Web Sites)

Orthopedic Foundation for Animals
2300 Nifong Boulevard
Columbia, MO 65201
(573) 442-0418

United Kennel Club
100 East Kilgore Road
Portage, MI 49002-5584
(616) 343-9020

*Note: This address changes annually with
the election of new club officers. Contact
the AKC for the current listing.

Rescue Groups

American Bloodhound Club, Ed Kilby;
(904) 788-0137. The national breed
club can direct you to a Bloodhound
club in your area that has a rescue
operation. The following groups
can also help place you with a
Bloodhound.

Bloodhounds West Breed
   Rescue
Susan Hamil
(714) 494-1076

Great Lakes Bloodhound Rescue
Jenni Osborne
9070 Eagle Road
Davidsburg, MI 48350
(248) 634-6426

Mid-Atlantic Bloodhound Rescue
Cheryl Slavnik
(804) 642-6930
e-mail: CSLAVNIK@ccsinc.com

Northeast Bloodhound Rescue
Julie Northshield
(518) 854-7010

NW Bloodhound Rescue
   Association
Adriana Pavlinovic
14002 Burn Road
Arlington, WA 98223-7182
(360) 691-4665

Southcentral Bloodhound Rescue
Walt Partin
e-mail: waltpartin@compuserve.com

Books

Some of these books may be out of print but can be found through book search firms, at dog shows, or through some Bloodhound web sites.

Brey, Catherine F., and Lena F. Reed. *The New Complete Bloodhound*. New York: Howell Book House, 1991.

Button, Lue. *Practical Scent Dog Training*. Loveland, CO: Alpine Publications, 1990.

Johnson, Glen R. *Tracking Dogs Theory and Method*. Arner Publications, 1975.

Pearsall, Milo, and Hugo Verbruggen, M.D. *Scent: Training to Track, Search and Rescue*. Loveland, CO: Alpine Publications, 1982.

Syrotuck, William G. *Scent and the Scenting Dog*. Arner Publications, 1980.

Tolhurst, William D., with Lena F. Reed. *Manhunters! Hounds of the Big T*. Puyallup, WA: Hound Dog Press, 1984.

Volhard, Jack and Wendy. *Canine Good Citizen: Every Dog Can Be One*. New York: Howell Book House, 1994.

The UC Davis Book of Dogs. Edited by Mordecai Siegal. New York: HarperCollins, 1995.

Magazines

AKC Gazette
51 Madison Avenue
New York, NY 10010

American Bloodhound Club Bulletin
Brenda Howard, Editor
616 Texas Street, Suite 101
Fort Worth, Texas 76102

Dog Fancy
P.O. Box 6050
Mission Viejo, California 92690

Dog World
29 North Wacker Drive
Chicago, Illinois 60606-3298

Video

Call or write to order the AKC Bloodhound video: The American Kennel Club, Attn: Video Fulfillment, 5580 Centerview Drive #200, Raleigh, North Carolina 27606; (919) 233-9780. The price is $34.95.

Web Sites and Mailing Lists

Bloodhound Bunch, http://www.bloodhounds.com/bhb/

The Bloodhound Bunch offers three mailing lists for bloodhound owners. For more information, e-mail dat@webcom.com

The National Police Bloodhound Association, http://www.westol.com/~npba/

NOSES-L, a mailing list devoted to scenthounds. To subscribe, send e-mail to listserv@mail.eworld.com with subscribe NOSES-L firstname lastname in the body of the message.

Index

The Bloodhound, famous in literature, art, and film as an intrepid tracker and loyal friend, is a great pet for the family that will train it, care for its health and welfare, and love it. The breed's incomparable sense of smell has made it the world's most famous canine detective. Its love and loyalty to its human pack is legendary, and it enjoys growing popularity as a jolly companion always ready to share a joke, a hike, or an evening by the fire.